YOUR HARVESTS

&

LEGACY

The Rewards Of Destiny

Book # 5 From The "Seasoned For Destiny" Series

Sally Mahihu

Your Harvests & Legacy

ISBN: ISBN 978-9914-9886-5-9

Copyright © 2020, 2022 by Sally Mahihu

P. O. Box 4317-00200 Nairobi

Mobile No: 0722 820 969

Published in Kenya by

House of Wealth Publishers

+254 737 405 827

houseofwealthpublishers@gmail.com

Table of Contents

Chapter 1

THE SEASONS OF A DESTINY SOWER..........................27

Embracing The Seasons Of Life

Chapter 2

YOUR HARVEST IN 7 AREAS....................................67

Your Harvest Is Well Rounded

Chapter 3

FACTS ABOUT YOUR HARVEST................................73

Understanding The Nature Of Your Harvest

Chapter 4

HINDRANCES TO YOUR HARVEST............................79

Do Not Stand In The Way For Your Harvest

Chapter 5

THREATS TO YOUR HARVEST..................................85

Brace Yourself To Guard Your Harvest

Chapter 6

HOW TO RESPOND TO YOUR HARVEST....................91

Your Harvest Has Ears to Hear

Dedication

I dedicate this book to every woman who has paid the price, run her race and is expectant of the harvest and rewards that are due to her as she leaves a lasting legacy for future generations.

Acknowledgement

First and foremost, I would like to thank God for enabling me to write and finish this Book Series. I pray these books will impact and bless many Women who are determined to fulfil their Destiny.

I would like to thank my **Husband Ngari** who really "gets me" and who I refer to as my "Destiny Spouse" because indeed he is a true gift from God and he has been supportive beyond measure during the course of my writing, these Books, in more ways than I can count.

My **sons Eric and Chris,** who are truly sons of my strength, and who have also supported and encouraged me in my "Destiny endeavours" no matter how radically insane I sounded at times.

My late **Dad, Chris Kahara** who constantly affirmed me and instilled the confidence I needed to embark on many "Destiny journeys" leading to where and who I am today.

Rev Teresa Wairimu, my "Destiny Midwife" who has spoken into my life for the past two decades and who has been diligent in nurturing, moulding and shaping me, to birth out the gifts within me (even during the times when my own foolishness and short-sightedness, coupled with a zeal that was often devoid of knowledge threatened to abort my Purpose and Calling.)

H.E. Madam Rachel Ruto who is equally passionate about the empowerment of women and who I admire and respect tremendously for her continuous and tireless commitment to better the lives of women in our society and Nation.

My Aunt Rev Judy Mbugua for believing in me and for being a pillar of strength to me for over the years as a Mother figure, for teaching me that my roles as a wife and mother are not an excuse for, but rather an incentive to fulfil my Purpose and Destiny.

My friend and Mentor Dr. Herta Von Stigel who came into my life, at just the right time and helped me to understand that I needed to conquer the Mountain within me before I could conquer the Mountains around me, and whose invaluable friendship and mentorship is a great source of encouragement for me.

My diligent research Assistants and Typists **Victor M. Mwangi, Frida Wanjira** and **Tecla Karimi** who all worked tirelessly in making these books happen.

My Publisher & Cover Designer Shadrack Radido of House of Wealth Publishers who allowed me the freedom I needed in this Series of Books even when I stubbornly chose to deviate from the traditional Book writing ethics and who has been a solid sounding board on the many technical issues regarding this Series.

My Editor Dr. Mark Stibbe for his excellent editing and no-nonsense professional approach, truly a gift in the literary world.

My die-hard Spice Girls and faithful Women from my Seasoned Woman Vision who cheer me on and whose undeterred insistent claims that there is still more in me for them than I let out, warms my heart and provokes me to keep doing that which I was created for.

Everyone else who contributed in one way or another to the conception and birthing of this Series of Books.

Foreword

I have known Sally for over two decades now from the time she joined and begun to serve me in Ministry. Sally is a very zealous and passionate Woman in whatever she believes in.

Beyond her professional career as a Lawyer, Sally has demonstrated strong gifts of speaking, teaching, mentoring and writing and over the years I have often encouraged her to unleash these gifts. I am extremely proud to see that she has finally done so in these Books **"SEASONED FOR DESTINY"** and I am confident that she will go on to author many more for the benefit of this generation and the generations to come.

Sally has a distinct Call to the Women in the Marketplace for whom has an undeniable burden, and her ability to reach out and offer herself to those women who suffer in silence, totally closed up, yet they really need someone they can trust and open up to.

Sally has addressed every type of Woman in these Books and the topics and subjects she has chosen to address are of great interest so she will reach and impact a very wide margin of Women, across the divide, locally and globally.

In other words, Sally has covered literally every subject that every Woman needs, to become well equipped and empowered for fulfilling Purpose and Destiny. More importantly she has done it in a manner that every Woman will identify with, because she has delved into the core basics of every issue without sugar coating the seriousness that one will require to commit to this journey to Destiny. Yet at the same time she has strongly encouraged every Woman by laying out the roadmap and by affirming and assuring her again and again, that she already has what it takes to master this journey and fulfil her Destiny.

Women from every sphere and sector will be awakened to the significance of their Callings and Destiny, giving them the incentive and motivation, they needed to forge on without giving up.

I have been in Christian ministry for over 45 years now and I have been humbled and privileged to minister to thousands of people Worldwide and to lead an organization with over 10, 000 partners locally and globally. The messages in these Books are central to the gospel that I myself preach because Destiny is God ordained.

I have no doubt that everyone who will read these Books will be greatly impacted and transformed, empowered and equipped to arise and lay hold of and fulfil that Destiny that each was born for.

Rev. Teresia Wairimu Kinyanjui.

Director& Founder,

Faith Evangelistic Ministry (FEM)

Endorsement

Destiny is one of the most misunderstood concepts today. Needless to say, the very mention of this word elicits feelings of inadequacy and anxiety among many. This has mainly been because of the complexity and mystery that seems to surround the understanding of what destiny is or is not.

In the 'Seasoned for Destiny' series, Sally wholeheartedly deliberates on the tenets that are to bring flavor and color to one's life. Reading through the pages it is clear that she empties her heart seeking to touch a heart at a time. This series specifically address the internal struggles that become stumbling blocks in the way of success for many and in particular women.

In today's world where everything is fast-paced and we all are confronted with many options; it is prudent that one finds their space and balance in life. Reading this book will motivate you to take a personal stock of where you are in the journey to destiny while recognizing and fixing the hindrances on the way.

To live a life of meaning and significance understanding Destiny is not an option but an expectation. As one who is passionate about women empowerment, I concur that clarity of purpose and calling, the fortitude to make available connections and the resilience to maintain success on the path of destiny can be overwhelming. This series is therefore an essential tool for one to make this valuable journey.

Her Excellency,

Rachel Ruto.

Spouse of the Deputy President,

Republic of Kenya.

Endorsement

I have known Sally from when she was about 5 years old and our relationship is firstly that of a mother and daughter. Beyond our family ties and now that Sally has grown to be a wife and mother with her own home, we have become very close friends and prayer partners and we are a great support and strength to one another in this journey to Destiny.

From an early age, Sally has demonstrated such a strong gift of expression and articulation. Sally is undeniably a gifted and anointed Servant of God who ministers the gospel passionately. She is also an inspirational coach and mentor to many women and girls from every walk of life. Her marketplace ministry has impacted many far and wide.

When Sally birthed her Seasoned Woman Forum about 7 years ago and as I witnessed her teachings, mentorship and coaching programs, I knew it would just be a matter of time before she consolidated those valuable teachings into books to reach a wider audience and sphere.

I think that every woman reading this book who will be transformed radically and propelled to fulfilling her Purpose and Destiny.

I am very passionate for Families and Nations, and a firm believer that strong healthy families are the foundation of strong healthy Nations. So as I read these Books, I was deeply affected and encouraged by the manner in which Sally has tied up the value of the woman, not only as a leader, wealth creator, professional, career woman, but also as a family oriented woman.

Any woman serious about fulfilling her Purpose and Destiny must be able to align her role as a family woman with her Purpose and Destiny and she must be cognizant of the fact that she cannot effectively impact Nations without first impacting families.

This series of books addresses every woman of every race, creed and color, and from any society and Nation, who desires to be and do all that she was born and created for.

Sally has adequately highlighted literally every dilemma and problem that a woman will encounter in the course of fulfilling her Purpose and Destiny, irrespective of her social status and standing in life, and she has given very practical solutions to these dilemmas and problems.

I would therefore urge every woman to read this Series of Books not only for her own equipping and empowerment but also for the equipping and empowerment of other women who she will share the contents of these book with.

Rev. Dr Judy Mbugua.

The Founder of the Homecare Spiritual Fellowship.

Endorsement

Sally Mahihu's book series "Seasoned for Destiny" is a clarion call for every woman, regardless of age, race or tribe, to discover her true identity, live out her deeper purpose and leave a legacy that younger generations are proud to remember. This book series is for such as time as this!"

(Dr Herta von Stiegel, author of *"The Mountain Within – Leadership Lessons and Inspiration for your Climb to the Top."*)

I am glad that Sally has followed through in writing this series of books titled **"Seasoned for Destiny"**. A couple of years ago, I gave her a word which I had received from the lord, that she would write some very significant books on issues pertaining to women in the marketplace.

These books will encourage and guide women greatly in understanding certain fundamentals that are related to their destiny such as business, career, leadership, relationships etc. Sally has captured literally every aspect of a modern woman's life, and she has taken time to address and analyze these issues in a way that every woman can identify with.

Sally has left no stone unturned in candidly addressing the subtle and not so subtle issues that often derail and delay many women from unleashing their full potential, to enable them to bring out their best selves.

I am persuaded that these books will change the lives of many women and will equip a new generation to become powerful agents of transformation in their spheres of influence.

Rev. Steve Pailthorpe

President of Crown Global, CEO of Iconic Digital & Senior Pastor of Crown Family Church

Introduction

I am fully persuaded that once a woman understands who she was born to be and embraces the reason she was created (the Purpose for her being), then she will begin to live purposefully and intentionally towards it, and attain true fulfilment. And in so doing she will not only lay hold of her own Destiny, but she will also impact and propel many people, societies and Nations to their Purpose and Destiny as well.

This Series known as "**<u>SEASONED FOR DESTINY</u>**" consists of 5 Books namely Book 1 Your Naming And Defining, Book 2 Your Calling And Positioning, Book 3 Your Relationships And Networks, Book 4 Your Making And Shaping and Book 5 Your Harvests And Legacy.

BOOK 1 titled "YOUR NAMING AND DEFINING" deals with a Woman's identity, understanding "**the who**" she was born to be, it addresses her ability to embrace her true and authentic self. The chapters in this Book expound the various fundamentals regarding Identity and the power of Naming; The Passwords to your true identity (understanding what should and what should not define you). The Triggers to an Identity Crisis, The Diary of a Destiny Diva, The Voices that shape and define you, The Destiny Queen or the Destiny Quitter, The Destiny Preserver or the Destiny Destroyer, The Destiny Clinger or the Destiny Kisser, The Destiny Connector or the Destiny Blocker, The Global Destiny Carrier or the Local Destiny Carrier, The Destiny Respecter or the Destiny Despiser, The Eagle Destiny or the Chicken Destiny, The Diary of a Destiny Diva and The Daily Confessions of a Destiny Chaser (on how to reinforce and affirm your identity daily with positive decrees and declarations).

BOOK 2 titled **"YOUR CALLING AND POSITIONING"** deals with a Woman's Calling and Purpose namely how to discover **"the what"** she was created to do, how to birth it and safeguard it, having a deep insight of what her purpose and calling entails, understanding how to access what she needs to fulfil it. This Book also it looks at the Woman's Positioning and Alignment on how to locate **"the where"** (in terms of sector or sphere) she is ordained to impact, how to navigate in that specific area and how to establish herself there. The chapters in this particular Book address the pertinent factors about Calling and Positioning namely; The Cues and Clues to her Calling, The Realities About her Calling, The Tools of a true Visionary, The steps to Birthing her Visions to Destiny, The Steps after Birthing her Visions to Destiny, The Pebble Stones in your High Heels to Destiny, The Arrows to her Place and sphere, The Snags and Snares in her Place and sphere, Establishing herself in the Place of Assignment and The Key Roles Of A Destiny Woman.

BOOK 3 titled **"YOUR RELATIONSHIPS AND NETWORKS"** deals with a Woman's relationships (networks and associations) namely **"the whom"** she should connect to, or disconnect from, for the sake of her Destiny. The chapters in this Book address; The Paradoxes In A Destiny Woman, Your Destiny Helpers, Your Destiny Killers, Your Sibling Rivals, Mastering The Art of Negotiation, The Spice Girls and Your Suspect Suitors.

BOOK 4 titled "**YOUR MAKING AND SHAPING**" deals with a Woman's moulding and sculpturing for Destiny namely "**the How**" of her preparation and equipping, and the various tests and trials she needs to undergo in order to fulfil her Purpose and Call as well as the principles, values and habits that inform her choices and decisions and refine her for Destiny. The chapters in this Book address and include; The Storms of a Destiny Survivor, The Scars of a Sculptured Woman, The Pain Patterns of a Destiny Champion, The Shape of a Destiny Diamond, The Trademarks of a Destiny Vessel, The Habits of a Destiny Addict, The Elegance of an Eagle Woman and The Pit-stops of a Destiny Racer.

BOOK 5 titled "**YOUR HARVESTS AND LEGACY**" deals with a Woman's legacy and the footprints she leaves behind for her generation and future generations. The chapters in this Book include; The Seasons Of a Destiny Sower, Your Harvest In 7 Areas, Facts About Your Harvest, Hindrances To Your Harvest, Threats To Your Harvest, How To Respond To Your Harvest, Reasons Why You Get The Harvest, The Purpose Of Your Harvest, The Marks Of A Destiny Legend and A Woman's Defining Decades. One of the main reasons for writing this Book was to consolidate the principles that I have been teaching, coaching and mentoring on over the years with regard to Purpose and Destiny.

Perhaps another compelling reason for writing this Series of Books is that every issue addressed here resonates within me personally, because these are issues I or people very close to me, continue to grapple with, and my sharing them here is for purposes of identifying my own personal struggles with those of the women I am addressing.

It is my sincere desire and hope that those who read this Series of Books will use the teachings to propel themselves to Destiny and to pass them on to other women, including those they are training, mentoring and coaching. These Books will also form very valuable material for discussion groups whether as Book clubs, diverse groups within churches, corporate organisations and in all the various sectors and spheres of influence and hence the reason I have inserted "Destiny questions to ponder on" at the end of each chapter so that the interactive discussions can have a real impact on each reader and hopefully provoke them to apply the guidelines offered here in fulfilling their Purpose and Calling.

My sincere hope and expectation is that these Books are going to equip and empower every Woman desirous of fulfilling Purpose and to edify and assure her that no matter how hard the journey has been and no matter how much she has wanted to give up, she indeed has what it takes to finish this journey because she was designed for Destiny and she is already seasoned for it.

Although the target audience of this Series is primarily Women, it is now clear to me that even the men who come across them it will be equally impacted and equipped by the universal principles and the various topics addressed.

It is also my intention to target the young woman (older teens and young adults) because most of these principles and issues will greatly help these young women to avoid the mistakes that many of us older women made in our early years, and it will hopefully help the young woman to also avoid unnecessary delays in her journey to Destiny. It is therefore my sincere hope and prayer that every woman, young and old will read this Series of Books and be propelled to her Destiny.

The most fundamental aspect when embarking on your journey to Destiny is knowing **"the who you were born to be"** and coming to a place where you embrace your true and authentic self and walk securely in it because everything else thereafter regarding your Destiny hinges on this first revelation about your true self-identity.

These Books address, every Woman at whatever place she may be in her quest for Purpose and Destiny, the late Destiny bloomer, the Destiny dreamer and Destiny chaser, the Destiny wagon, the Destiny spectator, the Destiny backslider.

These Women are all desirous of living purposefully but they each struggle with different aspects about Destiny, whereby some may struggle with knowing and discovering **'the who'** and **'the what'** they were created to be (their self-identity and Calling), they go round in circles seeking **'the where'** they were assigned to influence (their place and sphere of assignment) and **'the whom'** they were designed to relate and connect with (the relationships), many of them get blindsided by the how they get made and formed (tests, trials and tribulations), while others navigate life steering dangerously without a road map seeking **'the which'** (values and principles) they need to get there, while others become lethargic and burnout because they lack a sufficient conviction that the journey is worth the high price and sacrifice, they seem to be paying.

Every Woman's future after reading this Series of Books will be brightened by her assurance and confidence that she can now become the who she was born to be, do the what she was created to do, locate and position herself where she was sent to be an influence, relate and connect with the people that were assigned for her, surrender and embrace the process that will mould and make her into a vessel fit for Destiny, walk and align with the principles and values that she was intended to use to usher her to Destiny, lay hold of and effectively manage the successes, rewards and harvests that come with her faithfulness and diligence and leave footprints that will be a positive legacy for her generation and future generations.

What Is To Be Seasoned For Destiny?

For Purposes of this series of Books being "**Seasoned**" does not mean you have accomplished and "**arrived**" rather it means that you are passionate enough to lay hold of your Destiny, that you are ready to step forth by faith and embark on this epic journey just as you are; with the assurance that as you do so, the equipping and empowering you seek or need will be part and parcel of the journey.

… "**Being Seasoned for Destiny**" means that even though you occasionally struggle with who you are in the midst of a tumultuous dispensation that often seeks to swallow and drown you… YET you tenaciously fight to keep your head up, knowing that there is only one of you, and the only one you need to be, the one you were born to be.

… "**Being Seasoned for Destiny**" means that even though there are many raw and rough edges in your Character, that are still undergoing moulding and shaping… YET you continue to submit yourself to the skilful hands of the Master Potter, knowing that a "**Choice Vessel**" like you, will take longer to be formed because of the great impact and influence you will have on Nations and Generations.

… "**Being Seasoned for Destiny**" means that even though you have not quite mastered the Storms of life like failed relationships, chronic failures, loneliness, self-doubt and rejection, just to mention a few... YET you continue to brace yourself against those storms, choosing to dance in the rain; knowing that as you continue to set your sail in the wind of hope then ultimately, those storms will in fact become the very forces that will strengthen and propel you and bring you to that higher place of being alone, but not lonely, a place of self-knowledge, self-acceptance and self-assurance.

.... **"Being Seasoned for Destiny"** means that even though the seed of your womb has not germinated into the **"Daughters of Substance"** and **"Sons of Strength"** you had hoped for... YET you remain expectant that irrespective of any shortcomings in your parenting skills, or any unjust twist of fate, your resilience as a praying mother is never in vain and in due season, your Sons and Daughters will manifest into a Seasoned Generation, that will shake cities and impact Nations.

... **"Being seasoned for Destiny"** means that even though you may constantly be in a financial mess and distress, until you feel so desperate and drained... YET you refuse to despair knowing that your hands are anointed to create wealth and as you continue to trust, embrace and practice sound godly wealth creating habits and principles, then surely the floodgates of heaven will fling open and usher you into unprecedented financial freedom.

... **"Being Seasoned for Destiny "** means that even though the dire consequences of your **poor choices**, have come to haunt you and you are paying the painful price of your past folly under a heavy cloak of remorse... YET you keep your head lifted up high knowing that as you appreciate the lessons learned from your past folly, then this too will pass; because your harsh and ugly Winter must ultimately surrender to your soft and beautiful Spring that will come with forbearance and Second Chances.

... **"Being Seasoned for Destiny"** means that perhaps your inner joy is being dampened by the anguish and agony of a sick body.... YET you forge on, smiling through your pain knowing that as long as you have a Purpose and Assignment, that you are committed to fulfil and a Destiny to lay hold of, then your Creator will preserve you and keep you, until you are done.

…"**Being Seasoned for Destiny**" means that even though your walk with God is like a seesaw, characterised by some seasons of intense (almost fanatical) passion and commitment and a radical faith, but also with other seasons of panic, doubt, or even silent indignation when things do not go the way you thought… YET you pick yourself up every time and dust off the doubt and purge your panic, and with hot blinding tears, you make a decision to hope and trust anyway, knowing that He who began a good work in you is able to complete it.

…"**Being Seasoned For Destiny**" means that even though you have encountered Chronic failures and disappointment… YET it is about finding the grace to deal with the many disappointments of life and finding the resolve to regain missed seasons and lost opportunities, it is about finding the strength to reposition yourself for a new beginning, because a Seasoned Woman knows, that while there is life, there is hope and while there is hope, there is always another chance to rise again and forge on to fulfil her Destiny.

… "**Being Seasoned for Destiny**" means that even though you come to the end of yourself YET your find a song in your heart that keeps you going when the journey gets tough and this is the song that will keep her going even when the storms rage and the fiery furnace flares.

The Seasoned Woman knows…

Who she really is…

The Purpose for which she was created…

She is uniquely gifted…

She does not allow her failures…

And successes to define her…

She confidently says…

When I grow up, I want to be Me!

The Seasoned Woman knows...

She is fearfully and wonderfully made...

With a true beauty inside her...

Reflected in her whole life lived...

The Seasoned Woman clothes herself...

In dignity, honesty, integrity, patience, kindness, mercy and love...

The Seasoned Woman has learnt...

To embrace the seasons of her life...

Allow them to mould and sculpt her...

Into a vessel of strength, honour and dignity...

She is a Woman of all Seasons...

A vessel of strength, honour and dignity...

She has learnt to weather and survive the storms of her daily life...

Having the grace to dance in the rain...

To smile through her pain...

She has risen to define life...

The strength to rise like a phoenix from the ashes...

The Seasoned Woman has passion for her Nation...

She has solutions for her Generation...

And she has the welfare of her people at heart…

She is a voice to the voiceless…

So, as you reflect and take stock of all the myriad of Seasons you may have encountered so far in your journey to Destiny, remember that you are "**So Totally Seasoned**" for your Destiny and that nothing shall by any means prevent you, from finishing your Race and not only finishing it, but finishing strong… so soldier on **Woman of Destiny**, until you reach the finish line.

This Page Was Intentionally Left Blank

Chapter 1

THE SEASONS OF A DESTINY SOWER

Embracing The Seasons Of Life

Chapter Preview

1. *Seasons of Waiting and Preparation*
2. *Seasons of Equipping and Servanthood*
3. *Seasons of Sowing and Investing*
4. *Seasons of Transition and Change*
5. *Seasons of Threshing, Pruning and Purging*
6. *Seasons of Celebrating Others*
7. *Seasons of Victory and Breakthrough*

OPENING REMARKS

In your journey to Destiny and in the course of fulfilling your Purpose, you will encounter various and different seasons each intended to equip you and strengthen you in a particular way so as to enable you to fulfil your Purpose and enter your Destiny.

In the natural we have seasons where we see different patterns of weather. For some parts of the world, we may see winter, summer, spring, autumn and in other parts of the world we may see the dry, wet, hot or rainy seasons etc. When it comes to sports there are different ones which take place during different times of the year e.g., the football, baseball, cricket seasons etc. For agricultural seasons we have the sowing, planting, reaping, harvesting seasons etc.

A season is a period or a stretch of time when certain things happen appropriately i.e., the right time for the right thing; meaning that there is a season for every activity. Each season must bring forth its Purpose i.e., if it is a rainy season then it must rain, if it is the harvest season then a harvest is expected, if it is the baseball season then we expect to watch baseball etc. So too, the seasons of life that we encounter must accomplish their Purposes in our lives.

The important thing as we encounter each season is to discern the **nature** of that season, to understand the **Purpose** and the **reasons** why you are in that season, ascertain how you should **position** yourself and what **attitudes** you should adopt in that season, then you need to identify the different types of **people** you will encounter in that season and be wise in how you **relate** and respond to them.

"People are put into your life for seasons, for different reasons and to teach you lessons" ~ Selena Gomez.

And then you must look out and beware of the **dangers** and **snares** that come with each season, so that you can avoid and escape them. You will also need to adopt certain **strategies** so that you not only survive in each season but you also thrive and of course you must learn every **lesson** that you are supposed to learn in each season so that you qualify to **transition** to the next season.

There are other certain key factors about seasons that you must understand if you are going to command and work the seasons in your favour and to your benefit: -

- Learn to **embrace** (not resist the season) by adjusting yourself and setting the sail so you may flow with the season otherwise it may break you because you cannot change, prevent or manipulate a season.

  "You must take personal responsibility, you cannot change the circumstances, the seasons or the wind, but you can change yourself. That is something you have charge of" ~ Jim Ron.

- Learn to **balance** your seasons using your favours against your famines, so that during your seasons of plenty (whether it be in terms of material substance, joy and happiness, success and accomplishments etc.) you make sure you store up enough of that to get you through the seasons of lack, seasons of sadness, seasons of failure and dryness.

- Learn to appreciate the **uniqueness** of each season and see how, in retrospect each season adds you wisdom, growing and developing you for fulfilling your Purpose and Destiny.

- Learn to always see the **whole cycle of seasons** instead of looking at just one, and never judge yourself or others by one season only.

- Learn to take **advantage** of the **opportunities** in each season without wasting any.

- Learn to do the **right thing** in the **right season.**

- Beware you do not **miss any season** otherwise you will miss the opportunities that come with that season and you will have to wait until the next cycle of seasons comes round again.

- Learn to step swiftly out of one season and into the next to avoid being **stuck** and stagnating in any one season for too long. Discern the right timing for transition into the next season and do not procrastinate lest you get stuck in that old season and fall in the cracks between two seasons. Worst of all is indecisiveness where you remain with one foot in the old season and one foot in the new season. This will label you as double minded and unstable and hinder you from effectively fulfilling your Calling and Destiny.

"There isn't a single storm or season that we endure that isn't meant to mould us and shape us and make us stronger than we ever thought we could be." ~Unknown

There are at least seven seasons that will be significant in your journey to Destiny, namely, your seasons of waiting and preparation, your seasons of equipping and servanthood, your seasons of sowing and investing, your seasons of transition and change, your seasons of threshing, pruning and purging, your seasons of promoting and celebrating others, your seasons of harvest, victory and breakthrough.

1. SEASONS OF WAITING AND PREPARATION

"Good things come to those who wait" ~ *Unknown*

a) Nature and Reason for the Season

This is a season of **barrenness** where you will find yourself in a **dry place** where you are **unproductive,** where you are experiencing a sense of **emptiness** and **unfruitfulness** and you are awaiting for the fulfilment of certain promises or the manifestation of certain goals, plans and dreams that you feel have taken too long for example a business you would like to start or a relationship or a Vision or even a physical baby or healing from a physical ailment.

"The dry seasons in life do not last. The spring rains will come again." ~ Sarah Ban Breathnach

It is also a season when you feel hopeless, frustrated and like your faith is fading away and despair is creeping in and you are at your wit's end.

"Truly barren is a secular education. It is always in labour, but never gives birth." ~ Gregory of Nyssa

Understanding the reason why you are in this waiting barren season can help you wait with revelation and patience.

"Do not underestimate what God is doing during your season of waiting." ~ Unknown

Waiting can be extremely frustrating because you have done all that you know to do and you are not in control of how long the wait will be. You have a deep yearning so you are restless and nothing except that which you are waiting for will fulfil you.

"At the cry of a new born salt is being sprinkled at the wound of a barren Woman." ~ Unknown

The **reason** for this season is to prepare you for that which you are waiting for. So, your character, mind-set, emotions, attitudes etc. will be moulded and developed to mature and strengthen you. More importantly you will then understand the Purpose and value for that blessing. Other reasons for the season is to grow your faith, so that you fulfil and finish what you were created to do.

b) **How to position yourself in this season and what attitudes and strategies to adopt**

"Waiting well looks forward to the future while staying in the present, waiting well means I remain open to God and allow Him to move me towards the future He has planned in His time." Unknown

- One of the most important attitudes to adopt is **openness** and surrender whereby you are completely honest about all that which needs to be removed from you that could block and hinder what you are waiting for. So, evaluate self, analyse and do a self-stock taking of your attitude, motives, agendas etc. to ensure they are in the right place.

- *"Patience is not simply the ability to wait, it's how we behave while we are waiting." ~Joyce Meyer.*

- It is a season where you need to have **faith** and trust that what you are waiting for will surely come. It is a season when you need to remain hidden without too many voices and opinions.

- **Separate** yourself from the crowds, so that you may learn all that you need to learn from your

- Destiny helpers, (mentors, coaches etc.) including how to position yourself in this season.

- *"Sometimes you have to separate yourself from everyone and just focus on doing you" ~ Unknown*

- Separation helps you think, meditate, analyze where you are and where you are going and evaluate your past failures and mistakes, positively and learn from them.

- *"Waiting is always the season to listen and learn. God has some things to teach you before He answers your prayers." ~ Rick Warren*

- Another strategy is to **wait actively** and keep doing what needs doing, ensure that you are equipping yourself with right knowledge and learning all that you need to learn about what you are waiting for whether it be a business, a baby, a ministry etc.

- *"When you are in a waiting season, it's a season of preparation and self-improvement." ~ Unknown*

- Ensure to remain **connected** to the people of your Purpose at your place of your assignment and focused on your Purpose.

- Remain **expectant** and hopeful, without doubting that your season of waiting must eventually end and your expected end must come.

c) **The People you will Encounter in this season**

"Your mockers will only have your attention if you give them your attention." ~ Ernest Agyemang Yeboah

- You will encounter **mockers** and those who will taunt you because they are in their fruitful season and you are still in your barren season but remember that your mocker has no power to break your barrenness. So be wise and only allow the pain from your mockers to provoke you to press on even more passionately, but don't give your mocker your time or energy.

- You will also encounter **mediocres,** who will persuade you to settle for less than what you know you are entitled to and to aim for average instead of for the very best. Be wise and resist these temptations and patiently wait for your **"Isaac"** (the real thing) instead of settling for an 'Ishmael' (the counterfeit).

"Mediocrity is the worst enemy of prosperity." ~ Henry Ford

- You will encounter **doubters**, who are weak without faith and they will persuade you to quit and tell you that perhaps there was no miracle or promise after all. Be wise and distance yourself from such.

  "Doubters don't win, winners don't doubt." ~Isaac Bashevis Singer.

- Fortunately, you will encounter your **Destiny helpers** and encouragers those who will be instrumental in helping you to breaking your barrenness and ending your waiting season.

- *"The work that God does in us while we wait is just as important as whatever it is that we are waiting for." ~ Unknown.*

d) The Dangers and Snares of This Season

"There are no shortcuts to any place worth going" ~ Beverly Sills

- Some of the dangers in this season of waiting is **impatience** which may lead you to take **shortcuts** and to **settle for less**, or **giving up** out of **despair** and **hopelessness** and due to a **loss of faith** or **wrong focus**. So that instead of focusing on the people who have the power to break your barrenness, you end up focusing on the mockers, mediocres and doubters either in angry retaliation or in an attempt to explain yourself.

  "Never settle for anything less than what you deserve, it's not pride, its self-respect" ~ Unknown

- Other dangers are **de-positioning** yourself from your place of assignment yet it is the only place where your barrenness can be broken. Your greatest blessings will always come at your place of your greatest pain.

- In addition, **hardness of your heart** arising out of anger, bitterness and frustration and a grieved spirit will hinder your receiving, you may also get into the snare of jealousy because you see others thriving and bearing fruit which may lead you to **feel insecure** and **unworthy**.

  "The only disability in life is a bad attitude." ~ Scott Hamilton

- There is also the danger of **despising** and resisting the seasoning and your season of waiting so that you abort what you were waiting for.

  "Know that the waiting is not your ultimate home and resist the inclination to despise the season of becoming." ~ Rob Brendle

e) **The Lessons You Should Learn in This Season.**

"Our willingness to wait reveals the value we place on what we are waiting for." ~ Charles Stanley Ross

- You will learn to turn the **power** of the **pressure** from your mockers, doubters and mediocres into the power of your Purpose.

- You will learn the **power of right focus** on the right things, right places and right people. You will learn the **power of right timing**.

  "Always remember your focus determines your reality" ~ George Lucas

- You also learn the **power of intimacy with God** as you travail in the place of prayer, worship and praise.

  "Waiting will draw you closer to God or drive you away from your choice." ~ Unknown

- You will learn the **power in the wait**, from your season of barrenness, that being barren does not mean you had been forgotten, but rather that in your waiting things are working out for your good.

2. THE SEASONS OF EQUIPPING AND SERVANTHOOD

These are seasons of submitting under leaders and authorities and serving them whereby in the process you become equipped and imparted with the wisdom, experience and very valuable mantles from those leaders that will benefit you greatly as you fulfil your own Purpose and Destiny.

a) The Nature and Reason For This Season

In this season you are the **"student"** in **"school"** and there are **trainers** and **teachers** and you have come to a place that you need to graduate to another level in your journey to Destiny. So, you need a higher level of **equipping** and **empowering** and your character needs to be moulded and sculptured to a higher level, for greater responsibilities that are awaiting you at your next level.

Your training and equipping could be in any area of your life for example in Christian ministry, in entrepreneurship or corporate management and governance, in political leadership, as an artist in music or any other craft, as a media personality, author, as a mother and wife etc. The kind of training and equipping that you will require, and the kind of people you will require to train and equip you will all depend on what you are being trained in and for and the skills, competencies that you will need. Suffice to say that this training and equipping should all be aligned to your Purpose, Calling and Destiny for it to be relevant and valuable.

In addition, you need to get equipped through training and the harnessing and sharpening of your skills, gifts and talents, to a higher level so that you can accomplish more, impact and influence more. It is a season where you are not the one leading but you are the one being led, where you are not the one being served but the one serving, where you are not the one teaching but the one being taught.

Your training and equipping will usually be done as you are serving a leading visionary or any other authority in your sphere and Place of Assignment.

The Purpose of this season is to also teach you how to submit to authority, how to serve the Vision of another as you wait for your own, how to obey promptly and how to implement instructions correctly, as well as how to surrender your own views and opinions and allow yourself to be guided and taught. Submission and servanthood are critical tools that you will learn in this season and which you will need for fulfilling your Purpose and Destiny.

It is a season when you realize how little you know and how much you need to be taught.

b) **How to Position Yourself in This Season and What Attitudes and Strategies to Adopt**

The garments to wear in this season are **humility, submission, receptivity** and **teachability.**

"Accept corrections and you will improve and increase" ~ *Israelmore Ayivor*

- You will need a **capacity for feedback** because, it is also in this season that you will be **rebuked** and **chastised** and receive some of the harshest **corrections** and **criticisms,** because the final proof of greatness lies in being able to endure criticism without becoming resentful.

"Accept both compliments and criticism. It takes both sun and rain for a flower to grow." ~ Unknown

- You must adopt **unconditional respect** and **honour** for authority and for those placed above you to teach and equip you. You will receive and embrace your trainers and authorities, Purpose to see the value in them. Submit yourself with a heart of **servanthood** and receive the maximum impartation that you can tap from them.

"The influence of teachers extends beyond the classroom, well into the future." ~ F. Sionil Jose

- You will need to **cling** and **follow** them aggressively to ensure you do not miss anything they have for you.

"Admitting you need help doesn't make you broken, it makes you fixable and teachable." ~ Charlott

- This season of training is invaluable and you can only move on once you have acquired what you need for the next level of your Purpose and Destiny.

c) The People You Will Encounter in This Season

- There will be the **mentors, teachers** and **trainers** who will all command some level of authority over you whether they be spiritual authority, market place authorities or governmental authorities. **Luke 6:40**

"Anyone who teaches me deserves my respect, honouring and attention." ~ Sonia Rumzi

- There will be your **peers**, those who are also being trained with you, because they also need to be equipped and empowered for the next level of their journey to Destiny.

"Your training partners are key to your success and friendships based on your runs together are strong." ~ *Bill Rodgers*

- Some of these peers will be obedient and submissive but others will despise the authorities and reject the training and equipping while others will be encouragers and the others be defilers. Yet other peers will be the alumni (the former trainees and students) who have undergone this training and are now in their next higher level and they have a lot they can teach you, if you are willing. Respect the training, honour the commitment and cherish the results.

- Also, among your peers, there will be vicious critics who rejected the training and they didn't graduate to another level. They are stuck and stagnant unable to progress to the next level and these ones will seek to mislead you to keep you stagnant like them. So, beware who you align and surround yourself with, in this season of training and choose to focus on the reason for the season, learn your lessons and move on.

"There is no shortcut, it takes time to build a better, stronger version of yourself." ~ *Unknown*

d) **The Dangers and Snares of This Season**

- **Failure to honour and respect the authority** ordained to equip and impart you by undermining them. You may have contempt for your authority due to their age because some may be younger than you.

- Despising **their outward appearance,** because not all may dress sophisticated like yourself. They may also not have a command of the oxford English like yourself etc.

- **Refusing to serve** the Vision of another.

- **Impatience**, where you get tired and you feel like the training is taking too long. You may also reach a point you feel you have learnt enough and so you exit prematurely from your training and equipping.

- **Becoming offended** by the corrections and rebukes of your trainer, mentor and authority so you miss valuable lessons, and worse you remain stagnant in one season unable to transition or move on to the next level of your Destiny because you are not adequately equipped and empowered.

e) The Lessons You Should Learn in This Season

- You learn that **you are deficient** and you actually know very little compared to what you need to know for where you are going. You will learn that there are those who have the knowledge you need to usher you to the next level and there are no shortcuts because you must submit yourself to them in humility and obedience with a teachable spirit.

- You learn that **having gifts, and talents, is not sufficient in itself**, because they have to be harnessed, sharpened and discipled in the right direction. Raw gifts are very dangerous and can wound rather than heal, discourage rather than edify.

- As gifted as you may be, unless you are trained and mentored as to how you should use those gifts, chances are you may abuse them by using them in the way they were not intended, which will result in a lot of damage to either yourself or other people or situations.

- You learn that **you reap what you sow**, so if you sow submission, obedience, respect, honour, humility, servant hood and loyalty you will reap the same in your own season of leadership. Therefore, Purpose to intentionally and deliberately sow that which you want to reap later.

- You learn that **the journey to Destiny is a process** whereby you will need to be processed and seasoned to make you a fit vessel for Destiny.

- You learn that **your growth comes when hidden,** without much influence and when the use of your gifts is restricted. Even though your gifts are there plus your dream and vision, they are not yet manifested, or accepted as legitimate by others, because you need to be discipled. Your character needs to be moulded first before you can be entrusted to operate in those gifts, or in that business, leadership role, or have that physical baby or that marriage etc.

- You will learn **servanthood,** where you will submit under an authority and serve that authority as they fulfil their Calling and Destiny. In other words, it is your season of serving a specific person, organization or institution.

- Please note that every season of your life involves some form of servanthood because your Call and Purpose entails serving others, but there will come **specific** seasons when you are submitted under a **specific** leader or authority with a **specific** task and assignment, for a **specific** period of time and some of those periods may run into years. Suffice to say that even during these seasons of serving another's vision, you are also ironically still fulfilling your own vision, Calling and Destiny.

3. THE SEASONS OF SOWING AND INVESTING

a. Nature and Reason for this Season

The first things you must know is that you must sow in order to reap, just like you must plant in order to harvest. In the context of your life, you must invest either **physically** (as in your health), **mentally** (as in ideas, time energy and concepts), **emotionally** and socially (as in relationships, friendships and social networks), **financially** (as in business and entrepreneurship) or **spiritually** (as in your walk with God) etc. You must sow a quality seed in whatever area of your life you are sowing in so that you may reap a quality harvest or return. So, if you reap excellence, it is because you sowed effort.

You may have sown long years of study in a particular profession or discipline or you may have sown the seeds of the gospel. Conversely, you may be sowing a life of drugs, lusts and other destructive habits and behaviour or you may sow gallows for others to hang on etc. Just keep in mind that you will reap in the context of what you have sown. Also note that ignorance of what you are sowing does not stop the reaping from happening, so note the choices, decisions and actions that you are sowing.

"No decision will pay off more than prioritizing your life and giving extreme focus and energy to the things with the highest return" ~ Unknown

You must sow in order to reap. This is where you are spending wisely, choosing very carefully what you want to sow and invest in. Knowing that your return on investment (ROI) will be as per your investment and you will reap what you sow because everything produces after its own kind.

Psalm 126:5 – "Those who sow in tears shall reap in joy."

The **reason for this season** is to expand, increase grow and develop you in certain areas of your life, for purposes of fulfilling your Calling and Destiny. You will therefore assess which area of your life needs growing and expanding and sow and invest in that area or aspect because you cannot grow, increase and expand in an aspect or area that you have not invested and sown in.

Know the **right ground** where to sow and invest in, in terms of the type of business, concept, venture, organization, relationships etc. The ground is very important because you may sow into "thorny ground" symbolizing sowing into things that have no life and therefore your seed will be chocked to death or on "rocky ground" symbolizing sowing into things that are hard to penetrate, or on "reckless ground" symbolizing unwise sowing which will be trodden on and undermined with no chance of giving you any return.

b. How to Position Yourself in This Season and What Attitudes and Strategies to Adopt

- You must also **prepare the soil and ground** meaning by laying the proper foundations systems and structures before you sow and invest by removing hindrances and obstacles that could hinder your seeds and investment from taking root.

- You will need **faith,** believing that your sowing will bear the intended fruit and the expected outcome,

- You will need to be **patient** as you wait for it to grow because it is a process that takes time.

- You must adopt an attitude of **protectiveness** because you must guard and protect your seed from your enemies.

- You must carry out adequate due **diligence** and **research** regarding ventures, concepts and people that you want to sow and invest into.

- You must **nurture and nourish** what you have invested and sown by speaking, making positive confessions decrees and declarations of your expectations. Praying fervently over your seed and harvest. In other words, you must water and feed your seeds so they can grow "healthy" to maturation.

c. The People You Will Encounter in This Season

- Your will encounter your **Destiny helpers**, comprising of those who will give you wise counsel and advice as to what you need to sow and invest, where and when you need to sow and invest it. people who will ensure that you remain grounded and aligned to your Purpose and Destiny.

- You will encounter **supporters and burden bearers** those who will work with you by executing and implementing your decisions and actions.

- You will encounter **sponsors, funders and investors who will** provide the seeds (capital) ideas that you are sowing and investing.

- Having identified these people, your response to them is to embrace them gratefully and align yourself with them.

- You will also encounter your **Destiny killers** who seek to hinder and obstruct your sowing and harvesting. The way to handle your Destiny killers is to hide your seed, protect and guard it with your life.

d. The Dangers and Snares in This Season

- **Doubt and fear,** becoming impatient and losing your faith as to whether your sowing will reap a harvest.

- **Sabotage,** enemies and dream killers may seek to uproot what you have sown by using all manner attacks and devices.

- **'Tares'** thrown among your good seed in order to defile and contaminate it. "Tares" symbolize, the problems, negative narratives, false reports etc. that your enemies will throw at your seed as it is growing into a harvest.

- **Wrong ground,** when you sow in the wrong type of businesses, concepts, ventures, organizations and relationships, habits, behaviours etc.

- **Weeds,** these are self-inflicted as opposed to tares which are externally inflicted symbolizing superfluous, unnecessary, bright shinny objects, time wasting activities) that grow within your seeds and investments and that you must eventually uproot otherwise the weeds will suck the life out of your investments, and choking your seeds and hampering their growth.

- **Micromanaging,** the growth of your seeds and investments whereby you end up interfering and hampering the growth.

- **Shortcuts,** hoping to expedite the growth of your seeds and investments which will compromise the quality of your harvest and returns.

- **Adverse patterns,** keep in mind that sometimes, (out of no fault of your own) some factors can attack what you have sown to make your harvest fail e.g., adverse unexpected weather patterns, which symbolize circumstances and storms of life that catch you unawares.

- Take every attack and adversity in perspective and adopt wise well-planned strategies to damage control. Remain optimistic and in faith.

e. The Lessons You Should Learn in This Season

"Sow an act and you reap a habit. Sow a habit and you reap a character. Sow a character and you will reap a Destiny" ~ James Allen

There are at least 7 lessons that stand out from this season of sowing and investing.

- **We will reap what we sow**, whether good or bad. So be very careful what you sow or invest because everything produces after its own kind.

  Galatians 6:7 *"Do not be deceived, God is not mocked; for whatever a man sows, that he will also reap."*

  Reaping **what** you sow means that if you sow love and commitment into your relationships, that is exactly what you will reap and the opposite is also true.

- **The period between sowing and reaping takes time**, so you must be patient. We will always reap later than when we sow; our reaping will come in a different season, so we must persevere and not faint.

- **We will always reap more than we sow** just like a small mustard seed will reap a big oak tree, (even though paradoxically there is some measure of proportionality, so that if you sow sparingly, you will reap sparingly).

- **Timing is everything** in your sowing and reaping, so you must ensure not to be premature and not to procrastinate.

  "The harvest is for the appointed time." ~Lailah Gifty Akita

- **The quality of the seed/investment you sow will determine the quality of the outcome** and the harvest you will reap.

- **We must always protect and guard our seed** and investments from the 'birds' meaning our Destiny killers who seek to destroy what we sow before it becomes a harvest.

- We can reap from what others have sown, whether good or bad e.g., things sown by parents, governments, societies, leaders etc. which often manifest later in our lives.

4. THE SEASONS OF TRANSITION & CHANGE

a) The Nature and Reason for This Season

"When shifts and transitions in life shake you to the core, see that as sign of the greatness that's about to occur." ~ Unknown

Transitioning even where it involves physical relocation will definitely entail an inward process of upheaval whereby your emotions and mind-set are involved, so that beyond any physical move or change, you need to align your emotions and mind-set accordingly, otherwise a disconnect, will pull you apart in different directions and you will abort the transition.

"Any transition serious enough to alter your definition of self will require not just small adjustments in your way of living but a full-on metamorphosis." ~Martha N. Beck

Some of the most common reasons that provoke a change and transitioning are: change of **status**, advancing in age, a **career change**, a **role change** in society, a **shift in your personal beliefs** and values, **change in relationships, reputational failure** etc. and if you handle and manage your transition season wisely you will survive these changes and even thrive.

So, whether it be a change of a job position or loss of one, a marriage or a divorce, a change in financial or social status, a physical relocation, a death or a birth of a loved one, you are well able to manage it.

Always ensure that you weigh and measure the impact that every transition in your life will have on your Purpose and Destiny whether it will be a positive or negative impact so that you make an informed decision and manage that transition wisely.

Transition is a process not an event and it requires exiting the old, grieving and letting go, pausing at a place called neutral and then entering into and embracing the new.

Transitioning will bring you to a cross-road where you will be required to make some fundamental Destiny choices that will determine the success or failure of your transitioning.

Sometimes the reason for your transition is to move you from a comfort zone or a place where you are stuck and stagnant or a place that has dried up and it is no longer feeding you and you have outgrown it. Or a place where you are no longer productive where you have lost relevance, value and usefulness. So, you must transition so as to bring you to a place of productivity, relevance, greater growth and influence.

"Your life is a story of transition; you are always leaving one chapter behind while moving on to the next." ~ Unknown

b) **How to Position Yourself in This Season and What Attitudes and Strategies to Adopt**

- **Acknowledge** every emotion you are feeling and seek to understand its source.

- **Address and deal** with those emotions, respect the transition and avoid denial, because failure to own and master the transition means it will seek to own and master you.

"Transitions are places of emotional turbulence." ~ Amoding D. Oluka

In your Seasons of Transition, you may not necessarily be crossing over outwardly from a physical place but rather you may be crossing over inwardly from an emotional or mental place to another.

- **Align** your mind-set positively to the transition.

  "To change your life, you have to change yourself. To change yourself, you need to change your mind set." ~ Unknown

- **Embrace** and do not resist the transition. Trust your gut feeling and the innate wisdom within you to guide you, through the transition season.

- **Prepare and plan** so that you surf the waves of transition safely and smoothly and navigate the valleys of transition with light instead of darkness.

  "By failing to prepare, you are planning to fail." ~ Benjamin Franklin

- **Manage your expectations** as regards how long the transition process will take so that you adopt an attitude of patience and perseverance.

- **Put on fresh light garments** of strength, faith and courage as you discard filthy heavy garments of past pain and regrets: lest you obstruct or delay your "**crossing over**".

  "Seasons of Transition require courage and faith because you do not know everything about where you are crossing over to." ~ Unknown

c) **The People You Will Encounter in this Season**

During your transition you will encounter various people namely:

- **Your role models, mentors** and **coaches** who will guide you and give you wise counsel and hold your hand through that transition. Appreciate and allow these people to help because you will need them.

- **Old relationships** that you are leaving behind and that have been so significant in your life but you must now let go as painfully as it might be. So, in your seasons of Transition, you may experience deep pain and anguish because of certain people that you must leave behind not necessarily because they are bad but because their season in your life is over. Be radical in letting go of these people, otherwise they will hinder your successful transition.

- **Emotional resisters** i.e., people who are not ready to let you go and release you even when they know they must let you go. Be firm and move on anyway, no matter how painful.

- **New people** you will find at the new place you are transitioning to. Some may embrace you and some may reject you while others may be indifferent, towards you.

- Your response is to select your new relationships wisely ensuring that they are people aligned to your Purpose and Destiny. So that in your seasons of Transition, always understand **what** and **who** you must leave behind and more importantly **what** and **who**, you are crossing over to. Never forget those people who stood with you and prayed for you through to where you are because your transition into a greater place should benefit such people.

d) **The Dangers and Snares in This Season**

- **Resisting the change** by harbouring a negative attitude and resentment which will only make the transition more painful and protracted.

- **Failure to plan and prepare** properly for the transition will cause the transition to fail.

- **Your failure to manage** the stress that comes with change could literally paralyze you into inaction which could ultimately lead into depression.

- **Failure to emotionally let go** the **old** whether it be people, places possessions and positions will give you unnecessary emotional baggage which will make your transition heavier, harder and harsher.

- **Distractions** that will derail you in the transition, so remain focused on the process.

- **Getting stuck in between** seasons, perhaps the worst danger is failing to make a full transition, which is like having one foot in one season and another foot in another season which will split you. It is like having your physical body in one place but your emotions and mental attachments are in a different place, which will destabilize you.

- **Failure to be flexible**, adaptable and manage your transition carefully will affect your identity as it could cause an identity crisis.

  "Blessed are the hearts that can bend; they shall never be broken." ~Albert Camus

e) **The Lessons You Should Learn in This Season**

- Change and transition present **new opportunities for greater growth**, increase in possessions and resources, higher positions with greater influence and impact, new relationships with more value, all empowering you to fulfil your Purpose and Destiny.

- Change and transition allows you to **declutter and free yourself** from the old physically, mentally, emotionally, and socially and even financially which will enable you to soar higher into reaching your goals and dreams.

- Change and transition will give you an **opportunity to self-reflect** as to where you have been and where you are going, it gives you a chance to evaluate your milestones and missed miles.

"Those times of transition are great opportunities to look for recurring patterns in your life and make adjustments to build on the good and reduce the bad." ~ Dan Miller

- Seasons of transition helps you to learn the lessons from the chapter you are closing so that you can use those lessons to thrive at the new place you are opening.

- Remember that any transition, in whichever area of your life is easier if you believe in yourself, because it is not about becoming someone better it is about finally allowing yourself to become **the who you** were born to be, and to do **the what** you were created to do, **where** you were ordained to do it.

5. THE SEASONS OF THRESHING, PRUNING AND PURGING

a) The Nature And Reason For This Season

The nature of this season is such that you are undergoing a season of pruning, purging and threshing, to remove the unnecessary in you and enable growth and increase in you.

- **Threshing** is the process of beating wheat to separate the edible valuable part from the useless chaff symbolizing the painful process of separating that which is valuable in you from that which is superfluous and unnecessary, and even harmful.

- **Pruning** is associated with plants and it symbolizes, where some aspects in you have dried up and died and have become unproductive and need to be cut off and those other aspects in you that are good but have become overladen with excess baggage can be pruned to enable you become more productive and produce more.

- **Purging** on the other hand is a stronger analogy which is associated with removing the dross and worthless from the something. It symbolizes to cleanse, purify expel, eject, eradicate and rid something or someone from undesirable elements, patterns of behaviour and attitudes, bad habits, wrong mindsets etc.

- **Fiery furnace** this is a season where you are also undergoing the refining fire in the fiery furnace so that any further flaws in your character like toxic relationships, poor stewardship, dysfunctional social skills, lack of self-awareness, intolerance for suffering and sacrifice) can be dealt with lest they hinder you in your journey to Destiny.

- **Murphy's Law,** it is a season where anything that can go wrong goes wrong whether financially, relationally, career wise etc. The pain and humiliation during this season may be in the form of a demotion from a high position or status, loss of privileges, relationships, influence, credibility, respect, power, favour and benefits that you were enjoying, loss of reputation and credibility including loss of resources. Anything you hold dear in your life is shaken, sifted and sieved and it can be a very painful and distressful season.

Suffice to say, every one of these situations may have become a hindrance to you in your journey and after your pruning, purging and threshing you will be able to see these things in their right perspective and place them in the right place in your life with balance, and all of them will enable you fulfil your Purpose and Destiny.

b) **How to Position Yourself in This Season and What Attitudes and Strategies to Adopt**

- **Acknowledge** that indeed you need the purging, threshing and pruning in certain areas of your life.

- **Surrender** yourself completely knowing that it comes with pain but it will be worth it in the end.

- **Endure** the process for a fruitful and beneficial outcome.

- **Humble acceptance** of your shortcomings, weaknesses, your wrong attitudes, habits and behaviours.

- **An eager expectation** that as you endure the pain and humiliation in this season you will come to a good expected end.

  So, in short you should locate your place of threshing, pruning and purging and surrender yourself to it willingly, accept and receive the threshing pruning and purging and allow it to be completed without murmuring complaining or resisting.

- **Identify your Destiny helpers** who will guide you through this seasoning, so that you come out whole and not destroyed.

c) **The People You Will Encounter in This Season.**

  i. Your **Destiny midwives and mentors** who will guide you and coach you about the threshing floor. They will instruct you on how to lay down, surrender and embrace the threshing. Your response to these midwives and mentors is to follow their instructions obediently because they know what is best for you and they have been through the threshing floor themselves.

  ii. The **resistors,** those others who are supposed to undergo the threshing, purging and pruning but they have resisted it out of fear and disobedience. So, they remain stagnant without progressing to the next level of their journey to Destiny. These resistors will seek to dissuade you and derail you from your threshing, purging and pruning.

Your response to these persons is to maintain your focus and distance yourself from them because you know without pruning, purging and threshing you will not go to your next level.

iii. Your **judges and jurors**, who will condemn you harshly and mercilessly. In their view you must be the most wicked person to be undergoing this kind of process, suggesting that you must have done something to deserve it, and therefore you are not entitled to any grace, compassion or empathy.

Your should forgive these persons because they have no revelation regarding your Purpose and Destiny and the kind of processing and seasoning that you may need to undergo.

iv. The **blissfully ignorant** who have no revelation about Destiny so they cannot understand why you are embracing the threshing, pruning and purging instead of resisting and escaping it, your response is to maintain your focus and ignore this group.

d) The Dangers and Snares in This Season

In this season is you may seek to **avoid the pain** of this process by not surrendering and also by holding onto things within you that need to be threshed out.

The greatest danger here is **resisting** the season instead of embracing it or embracing the season half-heartedly so that you come out half threshed, purged and pruned and you have to undergo the threshing again and again.

Resisting the purging, threshing and pruning will only delay your journey to Destiny because the undesirable elements within you will constantly hinder you from moving on.

e) The Lessons You Should Learn in This Season

- You will learn that the threshing, pruning and purging is the **most beneficial seasoning** you can undergo in your journey to Destiny because without it you will remain stagnant.

- You learn to **let go of superfluous things that** you thought were necessary for you journey.

- You will learn that **our motives and agendas, need constant purging** to vet and qualify them, lest they hinder our production and fruitfulness.

- You will learn to discern between that which is necessary and that which is not necessary for your journey.

- You learn to discern the **things that hinder and weigh you down,** so that you resist and shake them off to avoid the painful process of threshing, pruning and purging.

- You learn that **the "threshing floor" is a place of separation and revelation,** a sanctification process, because within us we have wheat (meaning good qualities, traits and characteristics such as kindness, compassion, generosity, forbearance, love, hope and faith etc.) but we also have in us chaff (meaning bad qualities such as pride, selfishness, resentment, offences, despair, fear, past pain etc.) and there must be a threshing, so that the chaff can be separated from the wheat.

We also learn that **the threshing** is **a blessing** because it is the purified and sanctified part of us that enables us to fulfil our Purpose and Destiny.

At the end of it all, you will understand the power that comes from your threshing, purging and pruning and you will allow that power to propel you to the next level.

6. THE SEASONS OF CELEBRATING OTHERS

a. The Nature and Reason for This Season

It is a season where you are required to support and sow into another person's Destiny and celebrate their success even when your own success seems elusive, and you feel discouraged, disappointed and overlooked.

This is where you own Destiny seems to be on hold and the other person's Destiny is skyrocketing without any possible explanation as to why it is the other person succeeding and not you. It is a season when you feel short-changed as others go ahead of you and you are left behind.

In this season the reason is to teach you how to defocus from yourself and die to self-absorption and self-centeredness, and entitlement and trust in the process. You should acknowledge that perhaps you are not yet ready and if you are, then what is being checked is your ability to trust in the process without murmuring and complaining, and the maturity and purity of your heart and your ability to celebrate the success of another.

The other reason is to teach you that another person's season is not necessarily your season and that there is no need to be competitive and jealous because your own season will also come.

b. How to Position Yourself in This Season and What Attitudes and Strategies to Adopt

- In this season, you need to wear a **garment of grace**, because you will need to restrain yourself from feeling discouraged as you watch others attain their goals and succeed before you. Possibly these are your peers with whom you have measured yourself and you even feel that you sacrificed more than they did, so you'll need sufficient grace.

- Adopt **a pure heart** so that your joy for your peers is genuine and sincere and a garment of celebration for those others.

- You must position yourself with an **attitude of faith** and trust because you know that since you have been committed and diligent, surely your own season of harvest and breakthrough is near.

c. **The People You Will Encounter in This Season**

In this season you will meet various persons crucial to your Destiny such as;

i. **The stars of the season** who may hold you in disdain and arrogantly write you off as a loser because in their arrogance they have no idea that your own promotion is around the corner.

   Do everything in your power and might to support the Stars of the season, promote and testify about them to others and shed positive light upon them.

   Go as far as seeking wise counsel from them as to how they handled their journey, how they dealt with the challenges and dangers and what factors led to their success because these are lessons you can apply yourself to expedite your journey to this season.

ii. The other person you will meet is the **offended quitter**, one whose success and promotion has also not yet come but he does not have the capacity, grace and faith to believe that his promotion is around the corner and he therefore refuses to promote and celebrate the stars of the season. Distance yourself completely from the offended quitter and surround yourself with those like yourself who are able to promote and celebrate the stars of the season.

Beware that his negativity does not defile you. This is the kind of person who even resents and begrudges the success of the Stars of the season, erroneously thinking that the harvest and breakthrough of others denies him his own harvest and breakthrough, which of course is a misconception.

d. The Dangers and Snares of This Season

- One danger of this season is that you may be consumed with **resentment, jealousy, anger** and envy or even self-pity or lack of self-esteem or confidence wondering why you have not yet succeeded when others have.

- The other danger is allowing yourself to be **defiled by the offended quitter** so you also get offended and quit.

- You may fall into a victim syndrome and become stagnant and paralysed in one place or even become convinced that you are useless and unworthy and that maybe you have aborted your Purpose and Destiny and so you give up and quit.

e. The Lessons You Should Learn in This Season

- You will learn to be **others oriented** to be selfless and patient, supportive of other people so that when your day of success others will be equally supportive and celebrate you.

- You learn **the "bicycle parable"** that we each undergo different seasons at different times and if it is your time, it may not be my time. Like a bicycle pedal sometimes you may be up while others are down and sometimes you be down while others are up.

- You learn **not to compare** yourself with others and not to compete with others because another person's success and victory does not hinder yours.

- You also learn that we are each **running our own unique race**, with different instructions, different time lines and different rewards.

7. THE SEASONS OF VICTORY AND BREAKTHROUGH

a. The Nature and Reason For This Season

This is where you receive promotions into higher positions, financial abundance and returns from your investments, and seasons of sowing.

- Your relationships are at their best.

  Your family is thriving and in short, every blessing you could have imagined is pouring in during this season.

  It is a season when your tears are wiped away, your sorrow turns to joy and your night becomes morning.

  The reason you are in this season is because you have paid a price, you have endured pain, you have worked and walked faithfully with patience and endurance and finally you are ready to be rewarded and to enjoy the fruit of your labour.

  Another reason for this season is as a testimony to all those who mocked you, laughed at you and taunted you for pursuing your Destiny (something they thought was foolishness but which has now born fruit).

b. **How to Position Yourself in This Season and What Attitudes and Strategies To Adopt**

Ensure that you have all systems and structures in place lest you miss the harvest and blessings as they pour in.

- Wear the garment of thankfulness, gratitude, joy, humility and wisdom. Humility and gratitude because it has not been by your own strength nor by your own power but by the grace and faithfulness of God, and your Destiny helpers.

- Wear the garment of **tolerance** in accommodating those who have not yet reached their season of harvest and breakthrough so that you encourage them to keep running their race.

- **Identify the types** of harvest you have come into, in which areas of your life.

- **Adopt the right response** to your harvest.

- **Protect and guard** your harvest from enemies and be a good steward of your harvest.

- **Plan** how you are going to use your harvest wisely lest you waste it for lack of a plan.

- **Know the purpose** for your harvest and ensure you use it to propel you to the next level.

c. **The people you will encounter in this season**

i. The **begrudgers** are those who are also in their season of harvest but they have a misguided notion that the harvest may not be enough for everybody so they begrudge you for thinking you are reducing their share.

ii. The **discreditors** are those who have not yet entered that season of harvest and are envious that you have entered before them. They may want to discredit you and question you and question your validity for being in this season implying that you are not qualified or entitled to be here and that you got here prematurely or by dubious means.

iii. The **cheering squad** are those who will celebrate you and will help you to understand how to handle your harvest and how to be a good steward of it and these are the ones to embrace and let them guide you.

iv. Finally, the **enemies of your harvest** who seek to steal and take away your harvest so you must be alert and sensitive and to guard your harvest from them and refuse any of their deceptions.

d. The Dangers and Snares of this Season

- The dangers of this season are you become **complacent** and **comfortable** and you forget to be alert about the enemies of your harvest who catch you unawares and steal your harvest.

- The other **danger is pride** when you begin to feel that it was by your own might and strength that you got to this season, so you forget God and your Destiny helpers and you start living for self and abandon your Purpose and Destiny, and you forget where you were going.

- The **arrival mentality** fame and success coupled with the praises of men and the accolades may give you a big head so that you forget that your assignment is not over and that you have not yet arrived the final destination. So, beware of the **arrival mentality** where you forget that the journey to Destiny is not yet over.

- Beware of **"Spiritual Amnesia"** where you begin to forget where you came from and the days of your small beginnings. You begin to act as if you were always successful. Also beware, that you do not disconnect yourself from your Destiny helpers thinking that you will never need them again, forgetting that seasons come in cycles and that you will need these Destiny helpers in your next season.

e. The Lessons You Should Learn in This Season

- The key lesson you will carry from this season is that **patience and obedience** pays.

- The other lesson is that the **fulfilment far outweighs any pain or sacrifice** that you had to undergo in your journey towards this season, so it was all worth it.

- That **victory was always guaranteed** no matter how hard your journey was, you were not destroyed on the way because you are a child of Destiny.

- That **seasons come in cycles**, so even though you have reached this season of harvest and breakthrough, it is not necessarily the end of your journey to Destiny and after you have sufficiently celebrated and enjoyed your harvest, the cycle of seasons will begin again and this time you will be at a higher level of empowerment knowledge, strength and wisdom but also a higher level of challenges and responsibilities.

Destiny Questions to Ponder On

1. *What is it about the waiting season that frustrates you the most and how can you overcome this?*

2. *Have you ever missed a transition season and if so, what factors led you to miss it?*

3. *What were the lessons you got from your threshing, purging and pruning seasons in your life?*

4. *What is the most difficult aspect for you when you are in the season of promoting and celebrating others?*

5. *Which areas in your life currently needs the most sowing into?*

6. *What is the biggest threat in your opinion during your harvest season?*

7. *What have you struggled with most during the season of equipping and servanthood?*

This Page Was Intentionally Left Blank

Chapter 2

YOUR HARVEST IN 7 AREAS

Your Harvest Is Well Rounded

Chapter Preview

1. *A harvest in your Finances*

2. *A harvest in your Family*

3. *A harvest in your Health*

4. *A harvest in your Relationships*

5. *A harvest in your Spiritual Walk*

6. *A harvest in your Career*

7. *A harvest in your Calling*

OPENING REMARKS

"After the battle come the rewards." ~ Unknown

During the course of fulfilling your Purpose and in your journey to Destiny, you will receive and enjoy various rewards in terms of successes, promotions, material substance, blessings etc. as a consequence of your faithfulness and obedience. Some of the rewards will come at the end after you have finished fulfilling your Purpose and Calling.

2 Tim.4:7-8 **"I have fought the good fight, I have finished the race, I have kept the faith. Finally, there is laid up for me the crown of righteousness, which the Lord, the righteous Judge, will give to me on that Day, and not to me only but also to all who have loved His appearing."**

The 7 key areas where most women would anticipate and expect to receive a reward in are mainly in their: finances, families, health, relationships, spiritual walk, career and calling.

There will of course be rewards in other areas of your life but suffice that in some way or other they will be connected to these 7 areas.

1. IN YOUR FINANCES

"You need to treat your finances as a resource God has provided to fulfil your Vision, not a tool to fulfil your luxuries." ~ Myles Munroe

One of the areas where you will make an impact and definitely receive rewards is an increase in your finances by virtue of the fact that in your journey to Destiny you have continually sowed into your Purpose. A time comes where you must reap a harvest from all the seeds you have sown in the form of money, time, energy and material resources.

Chances are you have made great sacrifices and denied yourself and your family in order to fund your Purpose. Your good stewardship by denying yourself in order to prioritize your Purpose and Calling will finally pay off and after having passed the test of selflessness and generosity, you can now be entrusted with more than enough.

2. IN YOUR FAMILY

"Family is where life begins and love never ends." ~ Andrea Reiser

There will be families who you'll have encountered in your journey to Destiny who will have been greatly blessed and impacted by you fulfilling your Purpose either couples or parents with their children etc.

A time will come when it will be your turn for your own family to be greatly blessed and impacted. All barrenness will be broken in your family including healing, salvation, reconciliation and restoration of everything that had been taken away from your family.

Marriages in your family will be healed, those desiring to be married will be married, yokes and bondages will be broken and your entire family will thrive as a reward of your faithfulness in fulfilling your Purpose and Destiny.

All the sacrifices you made like being separated from your children and other family members will finally be rewarded.

3. IN YOUR HEALTH

"The greatest wealth is health." ~ Virgil

Fulfilling your Purpose faithfully, means that you will prosper in all areas of your life and be in good health and wellness even as your soul prospers. You will have wellness in every aspect of your life meaning physically, emotionally, mentally, socially, and spiritually.

Because of the many people who will have been healed either in various ways by the fulfilment of your Purpose, you will also reap healing for yourself and your loved ones as a reward.

When you have a merry heart, it does you good just like medicine and because your broken spirit will heal and your bones will no longer be dry. (3 John.1:2)

4. IN YOUR RELATIONSHIPS

"Treasure your relationships not your possessions." ~ Antony J. D'Angele

No doubt many relationships will be formed aligned or restored among people around you as you fulfil your Purpose. Many will have understood how to develop and maintain the right value-based relationships by virtue of your mentoring them and in the process, you will also gain valuable relationships etc.

Your own relationships will be rewarded and become full of peace, unity and value.

5. IN YOUR SPIRITUAL WALK

"Spiritual maturity isn't measured by how high you jump in praise but how straight you walk in obedience." ~ Unknown

As you fulfil your Purpose by witnessing ministering, preaching and teaching the word of God to your assigned people, they will grow in their spiritual walk by having a more intimate walk with Christ, a greater capacity for the word of God and a more consistent prayer life as well as the manifestation of the spiritual gifts within them.

Likewise, you will experience spiritual personal growth and your loved ones will also grow spiritually and fulfil the plans and

Purposes God has for them. Your reward here is the harvest of souls as well as eternal life.

6. IN YOUR CAREER

"Do what you love and success will follow. Passion is the fuel behind a successful career." ~ Meg Whitman

As you have been a ladder holder, sponsor, mentor for many to climb in their careers, likewise, a time comes when you and your loved ones reap and also climb in your career beyond your greatest expectations.

You will have Destiny helpers to propel you into greater heights and influence and doors of opportunities will open for you and you will be surrounded with favour as a reward of your faithfulness in fulfilling your Purpose. In other words, as you have helped others including helping their loved ones and their children etc. your reward will be that you and your loved ones will also be helped in your careers.

7. IN YOUR CALLING

"Nothing is as important as your Calling and Purpose in life." ~ Sunday Adelaja

The ability to fulfil your Purpose and Calling towards your Destiny is in itself a reward for your faithfulness.

In fulfilling your Purpose, you will have enabled many to also fulfil theirs and to become impactful and influential as they enter their Destiny. That commitment and sowing into the Callings of others will ultimately be rewarded as you also become impactful and influential and the jurisdiction of your Calling will expand.

Chapter 3

FACTS ABOUT YOUR HARVEST

Understanding The Nature Of Your Harvest

Chapter Preview

1. *Your Harvest comes at a Cost*

2. *Your Harvest is a Public Affair*

3. *Your Harvest must be Seized and Captured*

4. *Your Harvest Validates and Affirms you*

5. *Your Harvest is your Victory*

6. *Your Harvest will be Envied*

7. *Your Harvest will be Attacked*

OPENING REMARKS

Your rewards and successes will have come as a result of the fact that you paid the price, endured pain, made sacrifices and incurred certain losses in the course of fulfilling your Calling and Destiny.

1. IT COMES AT A COST

"Surely there comes a time when counting the cost and paying the harvest aren't things to think about anymore. All that matters is value, the ultimate value of what one does." ~ James Hilton

As stated in several sections of this book, fulfilling your Purpose will entail making some serious sacrifices for example giving up on other things you would have wanted to do, denying yourself comfort leisure and pleasure, disconnecting from several relationships that were once enjoyable, as well as enduring a lot of pain, suffering and hardship such as persecution, rejection, isolation, physical assaults etc.

2. IT'S A PUBLIC AFFAIR

"People are rewarded in public for what they practice for years in private." ~ Tony Robbins

Most of your sacrificing and enduring will have happened in private and because you will have had the grace to make the sacrifices and endure the pain and hardships. At the time of your rewarding and getting your harvest, it will be a public affair for others to see that it pays to be faithful and obedient and that every sacrifice will bear good fruit and that every pain will turn into power and that every suffering will become your success.

"If you want something, you've got to be relentless, people are publicly rewarded for the things they practiced privately for years." ~ Unknown

Because of your faithfulness a table will be prepared for you in the presence of your enemies.

Psalms 23:5 – You prepare a table before me in the presence of my enemies; You anoint my head with oil; My cup runs over.

3.   IT MUST BE SEIZED AND CAPTURED

"Success in life hinges more on seizing opportunity than having everything go according to plan." ~ Ethan Austin

The fact that you are entitled to a harvest and reward for paying the price does not mean it will come to you automatically but rather the rewards and the harvests will be available for you to claim and lay hold of proactively.

There will be many around you who do not want you to get your rewards and your harvests so you must be alert and positively aggressive and assertive in seizing and capturing your rewards and harvests.

Anything that is yours and valuable in your life, you will have to seize it by force because some of those around you will seek to take it away from you.

Matthew 11:12 – "And from the days of John the Baptist until now the kingdom of heaven suffers violence, and the violent take it by force.

4.   IT VALIDATES AND AFFIRMS YOU

"To validate: recognize or affirm the validity or worth of a person causes a person to feel valued or worthwhile." ~ Unknown

Reaching a place where you become entitled and qualified to receive harvests and rewards for your accomplishments is a milestone which validates and affirms you and your Purpose

It silences every enemy of your Destiny who had sought to obstruct, hinder or kill your Purpose. It vindicates you against every negative label, stigma and false reports.

5.   IT IS YOUR VICTORY

"Victory belongs to those that believe in it the most and believe in it the longest." ~ Randall Wallace

Getting a reward and a harvest for your Destiny is a clear demonstration that you have been victorious in the battle and that you overcame and went on to fulfil your Purpose and it is a testimony.

It is a sign that despite all the huddles and obstacles that were on your way and everything that could have made you give up, yet you held on to the end and you became a Victor not a Victim.

"Victory is always possible for the person who refuses to stop fighting." ~ Napoleon Hill

Your race was full of tribulation but you are of good cheer and you overcame the world and hence the reason you get the harvest.

John 16:33 – "These things I have spoken to you, that in Me you may have peace. In the world you will have tribulation; but be of good cheer, I have overcome the world."

6.   IT WILL BE ENVIED

"Insecure people put others down to raise themselves up." ~ Habeeb Akande

Your reward and harvest will obviously be envied by your Destiny killers and those who doubted your ability to fulfil your Purpose and more so by those who aborted their Purpose. Do not pay attention to such people and do not feel that you owe them any explanation for your harvest.

Proverbs 14:30 – "A sound heart is life to the body, but envy is rottenness to the bones."

7. IT WILL BE ATTACKED

"Don't depend on the enemy not coming; depend rather on being ready for him." ~ Sun-TZU

Beyond your harvest and reward being envied, it will be attacked by those who'd want to deny you your victory and snatch it away from you.

At the place where you become qualified for a harvest and a reward for having fulfilled your Purpose, it means that you have climbed to a new level in terms of your capacities, abilities, gifting, impact and influence and to that extent that new level will have "new devils" meaning new challenges to overcome.

Ps.3:6 – I will not be afraid of ten thousands of people Who have set themselves against me all around.

Chapter 4

HINDRANCES TO YOUR HARVEST

Do Not Stand In The Way For Your Harvest

Chapter Preview

1. *Self-Glory and Vanity*

2. *Analysis Paralysis*

3. *Fear of Success*

4. *Inability to Handle and Manage Success*

5. *Burnout and Meltdown*

6. *The Danger of Complacency*

7. *Amnesia and Dementia*

OPENING REMARKS

You must be cognizant of the fact that your rewards and successes will be opposed and resisted by the enemies of your Destiny and some may try to steal or sabotage your rewards and successes or to hinder you from accessing those rewards and successes. However, beyond those external obstacles are your own self-inflicted internal obstacles to your own Harvest.

1. SELF-GLORY AND VANITY

"It is not the mountain we conquer but ourselves." ~ Sir Edmund Hillary

This is where you are so excited about your reward and harvest which you certainly deserve but, in your excitement, you expose it to your enemies and forget to protect it.

In addition, you may begin to boast and take all the glory and credit for your harvest and reward forgetting those who helped you attain it.

Sometimes when you get your reward and harvest you become puffed up and prideful and you have the misguided notion that you attained that accomplishment and success all on your own. Beware of the praises of men and beware of allowing your success to go to your head. Always keep your successes in perspective to avoid the 'King Uzziah' syndrome (**2 Chronicles 26**).

James.4:10 – Humble yourselves in the sight of the Lord, and He will lift you up.

2. ANALYSIS PARALYSIS

(The 'deer in the headlights' syndrome)

"Thinking too much leads to paralysis by analysis. It's important to think things through but many use thinking as a means of avoiding actions." ~ Robert Herjavec

Whereby the reward and the harvest come as a shock and you suddenly find yourself in the limelight with all the attention and spotlights on you and you become unable to lay hold of your harvest and reward effectively.

Be expectant and plan for your success so that you do not become overwhelmed and frozen into inaction.

3. FEAR OF SUCCESS

"Fears are nothing more than a state of mind." ~ Napoleon Hills

You may be the type of person who fears success and therefore avoids it either because of the responsibilities that come with success or your fear of offending others who may turn against you because of your success, so when your reward and harvest arrives you subconsciously turn them down and refuse to lay hold of them.

"Procrastination is the fear of success" ~Denis Waitely

It is often said that failure is free in the sense that when you fail you are let off the hook from either being answerable or accountable for anything but success makes you accountable and answerable to that which you have succeeded in. This kind of fear of success is the **achievement phobia syndrome.**

4. INABILITY TO HANDLE AND MANAGE SUCCESS

"Can you stand to be blessed?" ~ T.D. Jakes

Many people when they reach their mountain top and receive all the accolades, harvest and rewards, become completely unable to handle and manage those blessings and end up losing them. This is due to lack of planning and lack of foresight.

This is because they do not have the capacity to handle **"mountain top experiences"** as well as they handle their **"low valley**

experiences" either because they did not really believe that rewards would come or that they would come in the manner that they have come. It is important to learn how to handle both our success and failures and it is a sign of maturity.

5. BURNOUT AND MELTDOWN

"Burnout is when long term exhaustion meets diminished interest."
~ Unknown

This is where the stress, agony and anguish that you have encountered to get to this place of reward and harvest have been so overwhelming that instead of celebrating and rejoicing, you burnout and meltdown and become completely oblivious to your success and accomplishments.

This is because you adopt a negative mind-set and a victim syndrome because you are still focusing and dwelling on the pain and suffering that got you there. This is the "**Elijah syndrome**" or **the Juniper tree paradox,** which is similar to the "**melted ice cream syndrome**" otherwise known as too little too late, meaning that by the time your comfort comes, your pain and suffering is almost inconsolable.

Meaning that by the time your harvest and rewards come you are too bruised and broken to enjoy them. The weariness of the battle makes you blinded to your victory. Beware of isolating yourself at this point because it could lead to severe depression. Beware because past pain can hinder you from enjoying your success.

6. THE DANGER OF COMPLACENCY

"If you always put limits on everything you do, physical or anything else, it will spread in your work and into your life. There are no limits. There are only plateaus and you must not stay there, you must go beyond them. ~ Bruce Lee

Sometimes when you get your reward and harvest, you become self-satisfied and smug and you settle there unable to go any further or any higher because you have become content with where you have reached so you resist any more challenges etc.

You must not relax after receiving your harvest and reward because there is always a new and higher level awaiting you which comes with its new challenges and demands so you cannot afford to sit back.

7. "AMNESIA" AND "DEMENTIA"

"Don't forget the people who helped you, get to where you are today." ~ By Unknown

This is where when you reach a place of reward and harvest and you completely forget what and who helped you to get there and you turn away from those people and place that were instrumental in your success.

Learn to appreciate and reward those who helped you, be a level 5 type of person who looks outside the window when you succeed to see all those who helped you instead of being the type of person who looks in the mirror when they succeed.

"Success often makes us look in the mirror while struggles make us look at God" ~ Unknown

This type of "Amnesia" and "Dementia" damages your valuable Destiny relationships and it denies you the valuable lessons you had learnt during your journey, thereby leading you to make the same mistakes.

In addition, having "amnesia and dementia" as regards the purpose for your rewards and harvest will cause you to misuse those rewards and harvest.

Chapter 5

THREATS TO YOUR HARVEST

Brace Yourself To Guard Your Harvest

Chapter Preview

1. *Abortion of Purpose*
2. *The Fatigue Syndrome*
3. *Trading your Purpose*
4. *De-positioning from your place of Purpose*
5. *Disconnecting from your Destiny people*
6. *Wrong timing*
7. *The Paradox of Hunger*

OPENING REMARKS

It is important to be aware of the fact that there are rewards and successes that come with faithfully and diligently fulfilling your Call and Destiny, because this way, you will remain motivated and you will remain alert and sensitive to ensure that you do not do anything that could jeopardize, prejudice or abort any of your rewards and successes.

1. ABORTION OF YOUR PURPOSE

"If there is no enemy within the enemy without can do us no harm."
~ Eric Thomas

This is when you fail to fulfil your Purpose for whatever reasons either because you were unable to address and confront the internal enemies within you or you were unable to overcome the external enemies around you or you were unable to pay the price because you rejected the process and therefore you quit before finishing your race.

Abortion of Purpose results from putting your gifts over character, yoking and aligning with strange things and forbidden relationships and touching the accursed things. It arises where there is a lack of fathering, rejection of authority and ignoring wise counsel from your Destiny helpers.

2. THE FATIGUE SYNDROME

"Fatigue makes fools of all us all. It robs us of our skills, our judgment, and blinds us to creative solution." ~ Harvey MacKay

This is where as you near the end and the final stages of fulfilling your Purpose, you become too weary or too wounded to get to the finishing line, and you quit on the eve of your breakthrough.

Fatigue can also make you behave irrationally and allow your emotions to get out of control and you make one single mistake and blunder that will cost you all the years you have walked faithfully and paid such a high price. So be cautious, sensitive and alert when you are nearing your breakthrough towards your harvest and rewards because that is the most slippery place.

3. TRADING YOUR PURPOSE

This is where you despise your Purpose or fail to understand its value or exchange it for temporary comfort or gratification and therefore lose it.

Trading your Purpose leads to an identity crisis because once you've given up your place and position you are in essence giving up your identity.

So do not allow short term gratification to cost you an eternal reward and do not make permanent decisions based on a temporary situation. Let the fulfilment of your Purpose and Destiny override any hunger or want that you may have during your journey.

4. DE-POSITIONING FROM YOUR PLACE OF PURPOSE

Your Purpose must be fulfilled at a particular designated and ordained place so de-positioning yourself prematurely before you finish your Purpose means you will not fulfil your Purpose. Your place of Purpose is your place of conceiving and it is also the place of your birthing your visions and Purpose. It is where you will carry the pregnancy of your Vision and Purpose in safety under the covering of your Destiny helpers who are located at that place of Purpose, so de-positioning from that place is tantamount to Destiny suicide.

5. DISCONNECTING FROM YOUR DESTINY PEOPLE

You will need crucial relationships to fulfil your Purpose so if you disconnect from those relationships prematurely, you will not be able to fulfil your Purpose.

Each of your Destiny helpers has a crucial role and assignment to play in your life and you must allow its completion otherwise you will be looking at a half-baked Purpose at the very least or a total Purpose failure at the very worst.

You must honour your Destiny helpers and the value they add to you.

6. WRONG TIMING

"Timing is everything. When you are really ready for it, it will come." Unknown

Seeking to reap before harvest time, is where you ignore the right timing and you prematurely seek to lay hold of a harvest or reward before you have become qualified for it. The weight of that reward and harvest is often too heavy for you if not ready and it can crush and destroy you. Greed can lead you to grabbing your harvest and reward before time and it can cost you dearly.

Remember that there is a season and time for everything so you must patiently wait.

"Be careful about rushing God's timing. You never know who or what he is protecting you from." ~ Karen Showell

7. THE PARADOX OF HUNGER

You have to be hungry enough to wait for the real thing because rushing to satisfy yourself with that which is fake (or a counterfeit) will still leave you hungry. It will deny you proper and lasting fulfilment. So be careful that you do not engage in a Purpose that you are not ordained for because then you will miss your real Purpose. In addition, that which is supposed to nourish and fulfil you does not come easy but because it is the real thing it is worth the wait.

The paradox here is that your hunger for things that pertain to your Destiny cannot be satisfied so easily and there is a sacrifice and a price to pay for those who are hungry enough to wait for their real portion.

Chapter 6

HOW TO RESPOND TO YOUR HARVEST

Your Harvest Has Ears to Hear

Chapter Preview

1. *With Gratitude*

2. *With Celebration*

3. *With Humility*

4. *With Contentment*

5. *By Managing it Well*

6. *By Treasuring it*

7. *By Sharing it with others*

OPENING REMARKS

Considering the toll that the journey to Destiny takes on you, sometimes when the rewards and successes come you may not be prepared to lay hold of them because you are probably still healing from what you have had to go through to get here, so it is important to keep reminding yourself and preparing yourself mentally and emotionally so that when the rewards and successes come, you respond and handle them appropriately.

1. WITH GRATITUDE

"Gratitude is the healthiest of all human emotions. The more you express gratitude for what you have, the more likely you will have even more to express gratitude for." ~ Zig Ziglar

It is crucial that you be grateful because it is by the grace of God and the support of many people that you have even managed to reach this place of reward. As you stand on the dais of success, be careful to bow your head slightly in gratitude as opposed to lifting it up arrogance.

"Create the habit of gratitude and watch your life transform." ~ Robin Lee

2. WITH CELEBRATION

"The more you celebrate your life, the more there is in life to celebrate." ~ Oprah Winfrey

Even as you must be grateful and humble in receiving your harvest and reward, you must nonetheless celebrate it without apology, because at this stage you are celebrating not only yourself but those who supported you to get there as well as celebrating the impact your harvest will have on many people. You are also celebrating the faithfulness of God.

3. WITH HUMILITY

"Humility is not thinking less of yourself, it's thinking of yourself less." ~ Rick Warren

You should receive your reward and harvest with a lot of humility knowing what it has taken for you to get to where you are and knowing the fact that there were many times when you thought you'd not make it but finally here you are.

Your humility should come from the knowledge that you got here by grace and that it is not because you knew it all or that you were so great and perfect.

4. WITH CONTENTMENT

"Discontentment shows up when we focus on what we can't have rather than what we do have." ~ Emily P. Freeman

Do not despise or belittle your reward or harvest either by its size of volume on the grounds that you expected something bigger or better. Your ability to fulfil your Purpose has equipped you with an ability to turn even the smallest blessings into big blessings and to work with what you have, leveraging and maximizing it.

Being discontented with your harvest and rewards demonstrates an arrogance and pride because you are harbouring unrealistic and misguided expectations or presumptions that are baseless. So be grateful that you may qualify for even greater rewards.

5. BY MANAGING IT WELL

"We must remember, we are stewards of what God has provided for us." ~ Joyce Meyer

Often unmanaged blessings can become burdens and you can become overwhelmed and weary so that what was supposed to be a blessing becomes a sorrow.

"The one principle that surrounds everything else is that of stewardship; that we are the managers of everything that God has given us." ~ Larry Burkett

It would be such a tragedy for you to have run your race so well and to have been such a good steward of the resources at your disposal to only now become unable to manage your harvest and rewards. So, learn how to handle your harvest and rewards by seeking wise counsel and advice from your Destiny helpers etc.

6. BY TREASURING IT

"Now is now. Here is my treasure." ~ Gretchen Rubin

As stated earlier your harvest and reward will be envied and attacked and therefore you must treasure it and protect it as something valuable that has cost you so much. The value in your reward and harvest comes from the price you have paid to attain it. Treasuring it entails using it properly for the right reasons and purposes.

7. BY SHARING IT WITH OTHERS

"When you focus on being a blessing, God makes sure that you are always blessed in abundance. ~ Joel Osteen

Those who helped you come to this place of a reward and harvest will include your Destiny helpers and connectors namely your midwives, mentors, funders, supporters etc. and who must become partakers of your blessings at this point.

Also share with those who did not help you at all as a way of empowering them and setting an example of generosity.

"I believe that God has blessed me in immeasurably ways so that I can, in return bless and help others." ~Karen Civil

Hebrews 13:16 – But do not forget to do good and to share, for with such sacrifices God is well pleased.

Chapter 7

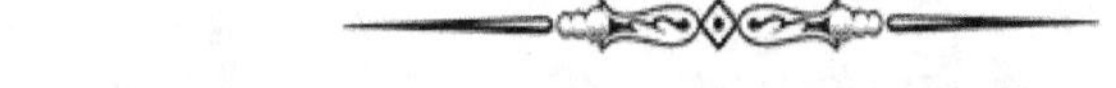

REASONS WHY YOU GET THE HARVEST

Knowing the Price Your Paid for Your Harvest

Chapter Preview

1. *For Winning the Battle*

2. *For Persevering and Enduring*

3. *For Competing within the Rules*

4. *For Running Purposefully*

5. *For Attaining the Goal*

6. *For Finishing your Race Well*

7. *For Winning with Discipline*

OPENING REMARKS

"Keep your eyes on the prize." ~ Peter Seeger

There is a manner in which you are supposed to fulfil your Purpose, by following certain principles and instructions and it is because of following those principles and instructions that you become qualified for the harvest. In other words, there are proper means to the end and the end must be justified by the means.

In addition to that end being justified by the means, following those principles and instructions will enable you to be effective and expedient in fulfilling your Purpose and probably avoid a lot of unnecessary huddles and set-backs.

1. FOR WINNING THE BATTLE

"After the battle come the rewards." ~ Unknown

You get the harvest because indeed you have fought the good fight, you have faced and overcome many battles on the way, you have not given up, because you walked by faith, and you kept your focus fixed.

This means that you remained alert and sensitive throughout, so that you saw the battles ahead of you, and you prepared yourself adequately by walking in the right habits, rising above and surviving the storms etc.

2. FOR PERSEVERING AND ENDURING

"Perseverance must finish its work so that you may be mature and complete, not lacking anything." James 1:4

Fulfilling your Purpose will entail passing certain tests, being patient in many tribulations, facing and overcoming many trials, coming out of your fiery furnaces without even a hint of smoke, surviving the lion's den, allowing yourself to be pruned and purged and surrendering at your threshing floor so that everything good in you can be separated and preserved and everything negative in you can be eradicated.

You have also gone through many seasons without growing weary and allowed them to mould and sculpture you because you knew that in due season you would reap if you did not lose heart and it is your rejoicing in hope through all these hardships that qualify you for the harvest.

3. FOR COMPETING WITHIN THE RULES

"So long as it stays within the rules of the game, which is to say, engages in open and free competition without deception or fraud."
~Milton Friedman

When you are fulfilling your Purpose, it is like running the race and you have to compete and you do so according to the rules meaning that you fulfil the right Purpose, connect to the right people, influence the right place and sphere and ensure that your Purpose accomplishes it's intended goals. It means that just like in a natural competition where you must adhere to the rules and even if you win but didn't follow those rules, you become disqualified.

You have qualified for the harvest because you have competed within the rules and you have won through righteousness. So, in attaining your goals and fulfilling your Purpose you were required to be temperate in all things so that the harvest you get is of a quality that is imperishable and will last.

4. FOR RUNNING PURPOSEFULLY

"Don't fight a battle if you don't gain anything by winning." ~
Erwin Rommel

Sometimes in a natural setting a boxer may lose the fight because he is constantly boxing the air without targeting his opponent thereby failing to knock down that opponent. Likewise, when we are fulfilling Purpose, we may fail to target the right giants and waste a lot of time fighting the wrong battle which is equivalent to beating the air in vain.

Also, when we are fulfilling the tasks and assignments within our Purpose, we may fail to be focused and spend a lot of time and energy working in vain leading to fruitless labour and leaving the tasks and assignment incomplete or poorly done.

We must therefore be intentional and Purposeful in everything we undertake. It is the fighting and winning smart that qualifies us for the harvest and for running within our lane. It also means that you are running your race and fulfilling your Purpose without confusion but with understanding and revelation

5. FOR ATTAINING THE GOAL

"If you want to be happy, set a goal that commands your thoughts, liberates your energy and inspires your hopes." ~Andrew Carnegie

The fact that you actually and eventually attain your goal when fulfilling your Purpose is commendable because many may embark on the journey and the race but never attain their goals.

So, your resolve to press on towards your goals with regards to your call and even when you know you have not already attained or arrived and you are not there yet but nonetheless you forge on undaunted to qualify for you harvest

6. FOR FINISHING YOUR RACE WELL

"Many will start fast; few will finish strong." ~Gary **Ryan Blair**

Beyond attaining your goals there is a further step of actually finishing your race, because finishing it is one thing but finishing it well is the more important thing because the harvest is not for those who begin the race but for those who finish well.

Finishing well means that you operated in a spirit of excellence and not a sub-standard mediocre spirit. It means that you did not leave a trail of people wounded and bleeding on the way side as you forcefully accomplished your goals successfully.

It means that you treated all those you encountered including your Destiny helpers appropriately reciprocating by also helping them to also accomplish their goals.

It means that you are appreciative, and grateful for all they did for you.

Finishing well also means that your Purpose will impact those people it was intended to impact and transform and that it solved the problems and dilemmas that it was intended to and that in the end it become a gift to your society and nation and it leaves a positive lasting positive Legacy to the next generation.

Finally finishing well means that you became a better person in terms of character and attitude.

Finishing well means finishing and giving credit and honour to God, as opposed to becoming proud and purporting to think you made it on your own.

In any race or competition not all those who are in it receive the prize but only those that run in such a way as to qualify them for the prize. Likewise in any task/assignment whether in a Vision, dream or project not everyone who engages in it is awarded or commended but only those who perform in such a way as to qualify for such award and commendation.

7. FOR YOUR WINNING WITH DISCIPLINE

"By constant self-discipline and self-control, you can develop greatness of character. Discipline is the bridge between goals and accomplishment." ~ **Jim Rohn**

Perhaps one of the most crucial aspects when attaining your goals and fulfilling your Purpose is the ability to remain disciplined and self-controlled, throughout because one of the most vicious internal enemies to your Purpose and Destiny is your flesh and carnality.

That ability to die to self and without counting your life as dear in comparison to your Call and Purpose. Subduing all your carnal desires and fleshly indulgences so that they do not interfere with your focus and commitment in fulfilling your Purpose, is what qualifies you for the harvest.

In addition, your capacity to rule over your own spirit, manage and control your emotions, maintain the right mind-set is what reaps in the harvest.

This Page Was Intentionally Left Blank

Chapter 8

THE PURPOSE OF YOUR HARVEST

Put Your Harvest to Good Use

Chapter Preview

1. *To feed others*

2. *To sow into your next level*

3. *To use it to become more impactful*

4. *To motivate and lift others up*

5. *To affirm yourself*

6. *To use it for birthing more harvests*

7. *Use it as a testimony*

OPENING REMARKS

Just like your calling and destiny is for a greater good, for purposes of benefiting other people beyond yourself, so too your rewards and successes are also intended for a greater good and to benefit others beyond yourself.

1. TO FEED OTHERS

(Allow others to glean from your harvest)

"Feed your soul by feeding the souls of others with love, kindness and compassion." ~ Daniela Nikolova

Your harvest, reward and harvest are not for you alone, and you should use them to feed and bless others, generously in good faith as you celebrate your success and victory, remembering that your Purpose and Calling in life is primarily about blessing and impacting others positively.

2. TO SOW IT INTO YOUR NEXT LEVEL

"You take care of sowing; God takes care of the growing." ~ Unknown

Part of your harvest is actually your seed into your next level, so you must use it to invest into the higher level you want to go to next. Do not eat your entire harvest but remember to keep some for where you are going.

3. TO USE IT TO BECOME MORE IMPACTFUL

The reason you are getting a harvest and reward is because you have been very impactful and influential in fulfilling your Purpose within your Place of Assignment, and consequently it is prudent that you use your rewards and harvest to become even more impactful and benefit more people and reach a wider sphere.

4. TO MOTIVATE AND LIFT OTHERS UP

"Motivation is the art of getting people to do what you want them to do because they want to do it." ~*Dwight D. Eisenhower*

Your rewards and harvest are also intended as a motivation for others to aspire to run their races as effectively as you are running yours, so that they may also get such rewards and harvest and in addition you can use them to help and build others by investing in their Visions and dreams.

5. TO AFFIRM YOURSELF

(To boost your self -esteem and confidence)

"Nothing builds self-esteem and self-confidence like accomplishment." ~ *Thomas Carlyle*

Your harvest is a way to remind yourself that you are valuable and relevant, to your society and Nation by the positive difference you are making, which in its self is a motivation and incentive for you to seek be even more valuable and relevant.

6. TO USE IT TO BIRTH MORE HARVESTS

Your harvest can multiply if you adopt the right strategies. It can birth even more and greater harvests for greater impact and greater benefit to yourself, your society and your Nation.

Your faithfulness and good works in fulfilling your Purpose will lead you into perpetual abundance whereby your harvest will continuously birth greater harvests.

7. USE IT AS A TESTIMONY

"True sacrifices requires sacrifice." ~ Unknown

Your reward and your harvest is something you must humbly speak about as a testimony to inspire and provoke others So that they may also endure sacrifice in fulfilling their Purposes so that they too come to a place of harvest and reward.

The greatest honour you can give to your harvest and rewards is by testifying about it but more importantly by testifying of the sacrifices you had to make to get it. Also testify about the lessons you learnt. That faithfulness, obedience, endurance, will always reap rewards in the end and that every storm you encountered in the journey was worth it.

However, be careful because sometimes there is a thin line between testifying and showing off. What makes a testimony pure and undefiled is because you remove all the glory and credit from yourself and you give that credit to whom and where it is due.

Destiny Questions to Ponder On

1. *Which area do you want rewards in most, is it in your finances, family, spiritual walk, career, Calling and why?*

2. *Which one fact about your harvest motivates you most?*

3. *What one threat to your harvest do you find most difficult to deal with?*

4. *Which one response to your harvest comes easiest to you?*

5. *Which one reason about your harvest encourages you most?*

6. *Which one use of your harvest do you find is most relevant?*

7. *Which one hindrance do you consider the most entrenched?*

Chapter 9

THE LEGACY OF A DESTINY LEGEND

Leaving Footprints for Future Generations

Chapter Preview

1. *What is a Legacy?*

2. *Why is it Important to Leave a Legacy?*

3. *Who Benefits from your Legacy?*

4. *How Do you Build your Legacy?*

5. *What are the Different Types of Legacy?*

6. *What are the Hindrances and Threats to Building your Legacy?*

7. *What are the Effects and Examples of a Good, Lasting Legacy?*

OPENING REMARKS

"If you're going to live, then leave a legacy. Make a mark on the world that can't be erased." Maya Angelou

1. WHAT IS A LEGACY?

Every woman serious and passionate about fulfilling her purpose, calling and Destiny should be cognisant of the fact that her faithfulness and diligence in fulfilling these will translate into a legacy for her generation and for future generations. It is therefore important that in our journey to Destiny we leave footprints and we use the bricks that symbolize our good deeds and actions to build legacies that will outlast us.

There are various keywords that you find within the context of legacy. We sometimes talk of someone having been a "legend". A legend is a story about someone who achieves an extraordinary accomplishment. A legendary person is a person famous for doing something extremely well. Being considered a *living* legend is most often an honour bestowed on someone still alive who is associated with admirable characteristics, but it can also be used about someone who has attained extreme notoriety, not necessarily for noble reasons. *Legendary* therefore refers to something or someone renowned, distinguished on account of a unique characteristic or skill. Usually, the connotation is positive, but not always.

The term "heritage" refers to an inheritance, a birthright or endowment. We often talk of a family heritage, meaning the background from which one comes. Heritage can refer to either your familial or cultural backstory. Our cultural heritage strongly influences our sense of identity, loyalty, and behaviour.

The difference between a legacy and a heritage is that a legacy is what you leave behind after you have gone while your heritage is that which is handed down to you from your parents - financial, physical (for example, your facial features), psychological (traits from your parents etc.), and so on. Legacy has a wider scope than heritage because it can be passed on to people outside your family, and has a longer application, continuing to the fourth generation of descendants. We should also note that "heritage" refers to the general endowment received by a nation from one generation to the next. "Inheritance" is the term used to describe the assets, estate, and possessions passed on by one's immediate ancestors, grandparents to parents, parents to children, and so on.

When we talk about legacy, we therefore mean *something that is handed down from one person to another - the footprints, imprints and blueprints we leave as an inspiration to the next generation.* This is not the same thing as your heritage. Webster's Dictionary defines heritage as something possessed because of one's natural situation or birth. Bruner and Ledbetter define it in a similar way, saying that a heritage is what is passed from parent to child, whether good or bad. This distinguishes it from a legacy, which can be passed on to anybody, related or not. A heritage is something you receive while a legacy is something you give. *You have been handed a heritage, but you will leave a legacy.*

Writing your legacy differs from writing your autobiography or memoir because the latter are simply recollections of our lives. Legacy expresses who we are and what we value, showing our mark on the world to build and benefit those coming after us. Leaving a legacy means putting a stamp on the future, making a contribution to future generations. Your legacy is your value to your society and nation, to your generation and future generations.

Here, then, are some questions for you to ponder.

At the end of your life, for what positive impact will you be remembered?

With what do you want your life to be associated?

How do you want to be remembered by your children, family, and friends?

What will those beyond your circle of family and friends remember you for?

What impact do you want to have on your community, church, profession, industry?

How will the world be a better place because you were in it?

What contributions do you want to make to your place and sphere of influence?

How will future generations benefit from your life?

Whose lives will you have touched and transformed positively?

What legacy will you leave? Will it be good, strong, lasting, imperishable, and eternal?

What story is your life writing for generations to come? (Remember what Steve Saint once said, "Your story is the greatest legacy that you will leave to your friends. It is the longest-lasting legacy you will leave to your heirs.")

What words do you want etched on your tombstone? Shannon Adler says, *"Carve out your name on hearts not tombstones. A legacy is etched into the minds of others and the stories they share about you."*

A legacy is accordingly something received from those who have gone before you. It empowers you to learn from the past, live in the present, and build towards the future, Legacy is something handed down from one person to another for future generations. It includes your significant achievements, exemplary service, and radical generosity.

Legacies are therefore the footprints we leave behind after we die. They prove that we were here, that we lived, that we mattered, and that we made a difference. These footprints are the impressions, impacts, influences, transformations we produced, whether negative or positive. They are the things that we leave knowingly or unknowingly, intentionally or unintentionally. These things transcend the places we have occupied and the spheres we have influenced - family, organizations, institutions, churches, social networks, businesses, enterprises, your nation, other nations - as you fulfil your calling and purpose.

Sometimes these footprints will be visible while you are still alive. To that extent you have an opportunity to erase negative footprints where possible and work on leaving positive ones before you leave by righting your wrongs and mistakes. When you bear this in mind, it becomes imperative that you are intentional about the footprints you choose to make in any place or with any people. Make and leave the right footprints!

How people think of you now is how people will think of you when you are gone because *today's footprints are tomorrow's legacy.* Legacy is your life extended into the lives of others and all the generations that follow. Perhaps the footprints that define you most strongly are those you leave in your specific sphere of influence as you fulfil your purpose there. This is the context in which you have been mandated to leave the right kind of footprints by deliberate design and not by default. Just as your purpose defines you, so does your ordained place and sphere of influence and the footprints you make and leave there.

After we have completed basic tasks like raising children and building our families and businesses, an emptiness may set in no matter how successful, how financially comfortable, and how empowered we are. Perhaps you have lived your life fulfilling other people's expectations and suddenly you begin to sense how unfulfilled you are. You therefore embark on a journey of self-discovery and you begin to be deliberate about how you live and the path you walk. This leads you to consider your legacy. Your legacy is how you will be remembered, what you leave behind to benefit others. It is the fruits of a life well lived and a purpose fulfilled. A legacy is leaving a piece of yourself for the benefit of others.

While fulfilling your purpose at your ordained place and sphere, your aim is to become a *living legend* because of the obvious positive influence and impact you are making there. It is therefore impossible to leave a legacy without having fulfilled the purpose and calling for which you were created, unless you are leaving a negative legacy arising out of your failure to fulfil what you are meant to do. Your purpose and Destiny will boil down to whether you make a positive impact in your generation. You should aim to become a history maker within your sphere of influence.

Your legacy is therefore your Destiny. Once you decide to focus on what you will leave behind, then you can become focused on your Destiny. Conversely, your Destiny is your legacy. What you are called to achieve is what you are destined to leave. This includes your significant contributions and accomplishments for and on behalf of others and your reputation – a reputation that continues to speak long after you have gone.

We all leave a legacy whether good or bad, by default or design. A good legacy is one which is helpful and useful in society. This can be an invention which is used today and will continue to be used by future generations. A bad legacy is one that leaves pain and suffering. This can be something like slavery. We often hear people say the following: "these scars are the legacy of chicken pox;" "their arguments left a legacy of bitterness;" "the war left a legacy of hatred;" "he left a legacy of huge consumer debt, political strife, economic ruin, and a fragmented society divided by racism and ethnicity." These are bad legacies. A positive or good legacy enriches people's lives and enhances future generations.

You have a duty to leave your sphere better than you found it. If you are going to leave a positive legacy, you need to know your core values and the principles that guide your decisions, you need to be willing to be a voice on issues about which you feel strongly, to have a genuine concern for people and their welfare, and a sincere desire for their lives to be transformed positively. By leaving a good, positive legacy, you are being a good steward of all that God has entrusted you. A legacy connects past generations with future generations, handing down the good that was handed to you and erasing the bad that was handed to you, so that you do not pass on negativity and destruction.

We should remember this: we can choose to leave a positive legacy despite having received a negative heritage. We may still feel the pain and damage of this negative heritage and yet we leave a good legacy because we make the choice to do so.

A careless lifestyle without a plan or purpose may cause you to leave a negative legacy by default (unknowingly) or by design (knowingly). You cannot escape those facets of biology and identity that tie you to your parents because no one has a greater influence in a person's life than a parent or a guardian. However, a negative influence does not need to determine how you live because you have the power to change it and to disconnect yourself from a negative heritage. The extraordinary influence of parents and other authority figures on children is obvious to all; such influence can mark a person for a lifetime. Men who were beaten by their fathers often beat their children. Women whose mothers married abusive men often marry abusive men. The cycle of pain can continue from one generation to another unless you make a deliberate choice to break that cycle and build a new and healthy cycle.

Some heritages are weak and fail to have the necessary impact, so it is up to us to ensure that what we pass is strong and long-lasting. Our legacy derives firstly from the way we live every day and the impact it has on our friends, our family, our community, and the world, and secondly from how we prepare others for life without us. This is a sign of our love and our consideration for them because we are taking the time to plan for the impact our absence will have on them. Remember, your legacy is not always about things; it is about who you are and how you touch and improve people's lives.

2. WHY IS IT IMPORTANT TO LEAVE A LEGACY?

i.   As a Memory

When you leave a legacy, you leave a memory of who you were and what you did. You should want to be remembered for something to show that there was a purpose to the life you lived - namely, to enrich people's lives. This is because future generations will embrace your achievements and try and emulate you.

Benjamin Disraeli once said,

"The legacy of heroes is the memory of a great name and the inheritance of a great example."

The best stories are grounded in principles and purposes that are timeless and certainly bigger than we are. Live a story that lasts an eternity and that leaves an impact on others.

Everyone needs to leave a mark on this world to know that their life mattered. So, understanding what you want your legacy to be can give your life meaning. It can enable you to allow the legacy that you are building to determine how you show up in the world each day. It helps you to live your life by design so that you leave a worthwhile mark.

ii.   As a Give Back

You should leave a legacy for others to follow because you also followed others who went before you who left a legacy for you. So now you are making sure that those who come after you will have a path to follow as well.

There are people who lived in a way that influenced our lives, shaped us deeply, for better and sometimes for worse. So how we live our lives is vital because we are shaping others. We therefore need to challenge ourselves; sometimes we may need to change how we live so that we can create the kind of legacy we wish to leave.

iii.   As a Sign of Good Stewardship

When you leave a legacy, you are being a good steward of what has been entrusted to you. We all have a duty to leave the world better than we found it because we shall be accountable before God. It is therefore our duty to create legacies that will propel those who come after us to higher heights - legacies that make life better for them. This is not about our own fame or recognition but about helping others. We are stewards of this world and we have a duty to leave it better than we found it, even if it seems like we play a small part. As Robert Baden Powell once said,

"Try and leave this world a little better than you found it and when your turn comes to die you can die happy in feeling that at any rate, you have not wasted your time but you have done your part."

To build such a legacy is a sign of selflessness. As Jim Rohn often says, "There is never a time to stop in pursuit of your legacy; there will always be time to do more, achieve more, to help more and serve more, so we should keep going and keep growing that legacy."

Legacy keeps you focused on the long term. It also gives you criteria against which you can judge your actions. When we are living lives of selfish indulgence and personal agendas, we are focusing on tiny goals. Your legacy is much larger than this. You should reflect on how you are going to use the powerful heritage you have received from those that went before you to build a life that leaves an even more powerful legacy for those that follow. What we do and how we live affects others. Our lives have the power to create good or evil, so it is important that we choose to do good.

iv.   As a Personal Fulfilment

Another reason why it is important to leave a legacy is for personal fulfilment. You want to continue your family's legacies and you want to be remembered for how you lived, not what you did at work or how much money you amassed.

You should endeavour to make significant family memories that will communicate what you believed and tell the story of your life. Leaving a legacy is a demonstration that you have fulfilled your calling, purpose, and Destiny faithfully and effectively.

3.   WHO BENEFITS FROM YOUR LEGACY?

Just as we benefit from the legacies of those who have shaped and influenced us - parents, family members, teachers, mentors - we must also benefit those we are influencing and shaping.

Keeping in focus those who benefit from whatever legacy you leave becomes an incentive for you to be more intentional. Generally, building and leaving a legacy is for the benefit of your children, family, society, the nations, and future generations.

i. Your Children and Your Children's Children

Your children, grandchildren, great grandchildren, and great-great grandchildren will all be affected by the legacy you leave. If it is a good and positive legacy they will benefit. If it is a bad and negative legacy, they may be negatively affected disadvantaged. Each generation passes on to the next some substance of their lives both good and not so good. We can learn from both, discarding the useless and embracing the precious for the next generation to follow, remembering the words of **Proverbs 17:6:**

"Children's children are the crown of old men, and the glory of children is their father."

ii. Your Family

Your immediate family members as well as your extended family members are also beneficiaries of the legacy you leave, especially where you have gone out of your way to build a legacy with them in mind.

iii. Your Society

Beyond your children and family, your community and society will also benefit from the legacy you leave.

iv. Your Sphere of Influence

Your sphere of influence includes your industry, profession, business circles and social networks. A positive legacy leaves an improved environment, an enriched welfare and transformed lives.

v. Your Nation and Other Nations

For some, their impact may go beyond family, community, society, and sphere to their nation and even to other nations.

4. HOW DO YOU BUILD YOUR LEGACY?

i)   Right Habits, Right Behaviours and Right Actions

You start building a legacy by eliminating habits, behaviours, and attitudes that dilute impact. It is not enough to add positive habits and behaviours; you should eliminate bad ones. Then, once you have decided what behaviours you want, you need actively to embark on acquiring them intentionally and deliberately.

ii)   Purposeful Planning

When envisioning how you fulfil your purpose and calling, you must identify the tasks, assignments, and visions you need to fulfil that purpose and calling. This will entail perseverance, endurance, patience, and long suffering throughout the process.

iii)   Seizing Opportunities

Lay hold of and seize small opportunities while you wait for the big ones to come. Stop procrastinating and begin to make a difference today. The impact you make as you live out your purpose, and the influence you exert and the transformation you induce, will define who you are, reinforcing your self-identity. Your legacy defines who you were and what you were about.

iv)   Living Intentionally and by Design

Legacy means that we aim to build into the next generation for their success. We influence people every day by what we say or do, what we write, what we create and share, and all this influence adds up. Learn to use the power of your life for the good of those you touch, from your own family to your communities and even your online connections. Live for others. The greatest legacies of history are left by those who dedicated their lives to the service of humanity.

v. Discovering and Fulfilling your Destiny

Discover your purpose and calling - what you excel in, what you are endowed and graced for, what you love and enjoy doing, what drives and motivates you. Then, begin fulfilling that purpose and calling intentionally, diligently, and faithfully. God has given each of us a Destiny to fulfil. Our world is ever changing due to the choices we make. Our hearts determine what our legacy is going to be because we make the choices to fulfil or not to fulfil our Destiny.

vi. Fearing and Obeying God

Our children learn by watching us live, so live with character, integrity, conviction, and passion, always obeying and fearing the Lord. The most indelible legacy is the way that we live and behave, so find out what pleases the Lord and live that way.

vii. Having Meaningful Conversations

Share family stories with your children because telling them can become a conversation they value well into adulthood. Spend quality time with your family. Give them the gift of time. Most children and grandchildren remember presence more than they remember presents. Learn to invest and commit enough of yourself so that your legacy is the fact that you loved enough to be there physically and emotionally. Converse and share with your children what kind of lives you would like them to live, even after you are gone. Let those thoughts constantly turn through their minds to help them navigate their own, crucial, Destiny choices. "What would Mum/ Dad do?" is the most powerful blueprint you can leave.

viii. Being Audacious

Be brave, bold, and courageous. Some people are brave and courageous throughout their whole lives, but others sail with the wind until the decisive moment when their conscience and events propel them into the centre of the storm. If you want to leave a lasting legacy you need to act with courage and boldness to reach out to those in need. This will be a challenge; it will require hard work, focus, habit. But if you want to make your life count, you know there is no cost too big, no sacrifice too hard.

ix.   Mastering your Legacy

Leaving a legacy is about being responsible. It means taking charge and control because no one will do this for you. So, define your legacy. Take the action required and fulfil it faithfully. Use a clear plan and an appropriate strategy that will help you achieve your goals and dreams. This will lead to the legacy you leave.

x.   Being in Love with your Legacy

Be passionate; serve in ways that make you come alive and that you really enjoy. Learn to assess your impact on others, what you are doing when you make the biggest difference. What do you do that makes the biggest impact on people, transforming their lives positively? Do more of that! Identify, develop, harness, and maximise your talents, strengths, and skills to that end. Know yourself and move yourself towards creating a positive impact by unleashing your full potential, your best self.

xi.   Speculating your End

Imagining what your eulogy will be can help you to define your legacy. This creates a radical, powerful shift in your perspective to achieve what you set out to achieve.

xii.   Believing in your Legacy

In addition, you need to be persuaded and convinced that you need to leave a legacy because when you absolutely know something is true, you become energised and activated towards achieving it.

Fulfilling your Destiny and leaving a legacy should become one of your unshakable convictions. As Dr Billy Graham once said,

"Our days are numbered. One of the primary goals in our lives should be to prepare for our last day. The legacy we leave is not just in our possessions but in the quality of our lives. What preparations should we be making now? The greatest waste in all of our earth, which cannot be recycled or reclaimed, is our waste of the time that God has given us each day."

xiii.   Being Others-Oriented

Put the needs of others over your own; be others-oriented and others-focused, not self-oriented and self-focused. Recognise the world's needs and respond with compassion and action. Help others to become better stewards of their gifts and abilities because this, and walking with conviction, leads to making a positive impact and influence.

xiv.   Being Tenacious and Resilient

You must keep going without quitting. The biggest regret in life is wasted potential so do not quit. You cannot give up or else you will not achieve your legacy and you will not become who you want to be.

xv.   Taking Actions to Actualize your Intentions

Ralph Waldo Emerson once said, *"To leave this world a bit better, whether by a healthy child, a garden patch, or a redeemed social condition, to know even one life has breathed easier because you have lived. This is to have succeeded."*

In the light of that, consider the following actions:

- Bequeath money to charities that are near and dear to your heart, and to visions and causes that you believe in
- Invest in the ideas and innovations of young entrepreneurs
- Create a scholarship at your former school for future students
- Start a foundation or trust and invest your resources, whether monetary or non-monetary, to benefit a targeted group of your choice
- Build and promote a sector or industry that you have a burden and passion for, with resources or programmes
- Establish centres for boys and girls, the elderly, the disabled, or a halfway house for those recovering from abuse, a rescue centre for young pregnant mothers
- Pass down handmade items and crafts, or start a new programme in your community, like recycling programmes, establishing cottage industries or ones imparting technical knowledge. The possibilities are endless
- Pass down skills and know-how in formal structured programmes
- Learn to record defining moments like births, weddings etc.
- Mark achievements and milestones because when you are gone, the records will be priceless. Be honest; nothing communicates like authenticity. Share your failings as well as your triumphs
- Add knowledge to your field or areas of expertise so that you leave a legacy through your body of work
- Write articles or a book
- Start a business or a non-profit organization
- Write your memoir; you can also record video messages for your loved ones, create a scrapbook for them or create a website dedicated to your legacy or even start a blog.

Remember what the great novelist Ray Bradbury once said, ***"Everyone must leave something behind when he dies, my*** *grandfather said. A child or a book or a painting or a wall built or a pair of shoes made. Or a garden planted. Something your hand touched some way so your soul has somewhere to go when you die, and when people look at that tree or that flower you planted, you are there."*

xvi.   Not Waiting, Doing it Now

Overcome procrastination and every mental block and get thinking about what you wish to leave behind by clearing away the clutter, whether in your physical space, or emotionally, mentally, financially, socially, or spiritually. Have a clear and decisive mentality.

xvii.   Putting Value, Time, and Energy into What Matters

Start now to live in the way you will be remembered. Knowing what you want your legacy to be will allow you to make better use of your time and other resources towards building that legacy. It will influence your day-to-day decisions in a positive way, keeping in mind that a legacy is not a resumé or list of accomplishments; it is the imprint you leave on the future.

xviii.   Breaking Past Bad Cycles and Patterns

In evaluating your heritage, it is important to understand and pass down the good aspects of what was handed to you. It is equally important to break the cycle of hurt and to create a new and healthy heritage for the next generation. Our aim, role, and responsibility as parents is to pass on all the good aspects of our lives to the next generation and break all toxic patterns of pain from the past by leaving the bad behind and disconnecting ourselves completely from it. Connecting past generations to future generations involves sieving the good from the bad, so that you hand down only the good, eradicating the bad. In **Ezekiel 18**, God makes it clear that a person's heritage does not determine his or her Destiny because every individual has the choice to ignore a good and godly heritage and follow an ungodly and bad heritage. Don't live in victim mode. Choose to rise above your negative heritage and be a victor instead.

xix.   Spending Quality Time with Those you Wish to Influence

Start with those closest to you and the ones you spend most time with, such as family and friends. No one has greater influence on a person's life than a parent or guardian. Embody the habits and behaviours that you would like your children, your family, and those close to you to embrace. Be consistent with rules and have consequences for breaking them. As you seek to influence and impact others, identify their key strengths and weaknesses, their successes and failures. Help them to learn from their mistakes and to discover how to move forward beyond every failure. In addition, document your values and your advice to your children and others; this is another way of passing on valuable lessons to the next generation.

xx.   Being a Role Model

When you serve as a good role model, you are leaving a meaningful legacy. As we age, we want to give back to the community by coaching, mentoring, even sponsoring needy children, sharing memories and wise lessons. This may mean making a meaningful plan for bequeathing gifts - one which can be implemented to benefit others long after you are gone. You can make it your pursuit to teach others the philosophies and actions that would help them achieve greatness and personal fulfilment in their own lives. You can help others achieve all their dreams. That is one of the legacies you can leave. A person can leave a legacy of good deeds like acts of kindness, loving service, and caregiving which is as valuable as any other legacy that empowers and positively transforms the lives of others.

5. WHAT ARE THE DIFFERENT TYPES OF LEGACY?

Let us consider the kinds of legacy we can leave.

i)   Good or Bad, Positive or Negative

As I have already stated, a legacy can be good or bad. A good legacy has a positive resonance in the minds of people and they often talk about it. It is also usually celebrated and honoured whereas a bad legacy is one which people want to forget.

ii)   Short-term or Long-Lasting

A legacy can also be short lived or long-lasting depending on its strength and foundations. Your aim should be to leave a good and strong, long-lasting legacy. Your legacy should be enduring, rich and precious. As William James once said,

"The great use of life is to spend it for something that will outlast it."

iii)   Material or Non-Material

Your legacy should be about far more than material things. Learn to leave a heritage, not just an inheritance. You should not leave behind only tangible items, like buildings, money, and possessions. Remember what Dr Billy Graham once said: ***"The legacy we leave is not just in our possessions, but in the quality of our lives."***

Some legacies are tangible - like children, artworks, crafts, poetry, heirlooms etc. - while others are financial - including endowments, charitable donations and even corporations - and others are the fruits of a life well lived. A life well lived is more about impact and love and less about material substance. It is having friends and family that love you and make a positive impact on society, as opposed to accumulating a lot of wealth, personal fame, and success that only benefits you. It is good to leave money for your descendants as a foundation on which they can build their financial futures. Make sure you don't just leave worldly material possessions otherwise your legacy will be worn out and broken by the time your path has ended. Aim to pass on things that are more eternal.

iv)   Children as Legacy

The pathways, guidance, life experiences, and life lessons that you imparted to them are priceless. Here is Dr Billy Graham again: ***"The greatest legacy one can pass on to one's children and grandchildren is not money or other things accumulated in one's life, but rather a legacy of character and faith."***

You should preserve your legacy by putting your values into words as a special gift to your loved ones and future generations. This can be limited to your children or extended to benefit people beyond your family.

v)   A Documented Legacy

Write down everything you would love to tell your loved ones, if you knew you didn't have long to live. Be sure to capture the essence of who you are by writing about your life lessons, values, accomplishments, and hopes. Think of it as an emotional heritage. Remember what C.K. Webb once said about the art and act of writing your story.

"A writer does not dream of riches and fame, though those things are nice. A true writer longs to leave behind a piece of themselves, something that withstands the test of time and is passed down for generations."

vi)   A Mother's Legacy

Someone once said that a mother hands over the baton to the next in line to leave a godly legacy to the next generation. If you are a mum, you must encourage your children, because the next generation needs inspiration if it is to be strong.

Leaving a godly legacy to the next generation means equipping them, sharing your plans, expertise, experience, and energy.

Leaving a godly legacy to the next generation means empowering them to be strong and of good courage and not to be fearful.

Leaving a godly legacy for the next generation means positioning them for success by giving them the platforms they need to make their voices heard.

Leaving a godly legacy to the next generation means publicly reaffirming them; loaning them your influence, telling them that God's hand is on their life.

Leaving a godly legacy to the next generation means reminding them that there is work left for them to do, being honest with them, teaching them that struggle is necessary for developing strength. Do not downplay the challenges of life.

Leaving a godly legacy to the next generation means pointing them to Jesus because He is the one who reveals our higher purpose and higher calling in life.

Leaving a godly legacy to the next generation means reassuring them that they have what it takes to make it.

Leaving a godly legacy means releasing them to leave home and make their own space in the world and make their own difference and leave their own mark.

Leaving a godly legacy to the next generation means rejoicing with them, celebrating their successes, and helping them to put their failures in perspective.

In addition to these, there are other types of legacy:

- **Cultural** – these are social conventions, norms, traditions, and practices. Our duty is to pass on the good ones and not the abominable ones.

- **Moral** – every culture develops good and bad ethics. For example, prostitution is an unethical practice. Our job is to hand down the good and reject the bad.

- **Financial** – for example, charitable donations to the poor to address their needs, improve their welfare and give them a chance to become self-reliant.

- **Historical** – explaining the origin of a phenomenon or how something came to be. We need to pass on good traditions while rejecting outmoded, unhealthy ones.

- **Scientific** – we pass on the scientific innovations and advances that we enjoy today, such as the cure for various diseases like malaria.

- **Political** - presidents and prime ministers often speak of leaving a social impact upon future generations.

- **Educational** - some educators who never had children have parented millions, motivating others towards love, kindness, and compassion.

- **Spiritual** - the best legacy we can leave is a godly one because it has the power to give birth to a positive emotional, social, and financial heritage. Remember what Paul said to Timothy in 1

Timothy 4:8: "For bodily exercise profits a little, but godliness is profitable for all things, having promise of the life that now is and of that which is to come."

Following Biblical principles, you leave an inheritance that affects the eternal destinies of those that come after you.

It is hard not to understate the importance of the last of these (spiritual legacy). Some inheritances include houses, lands, and money, but far more precious are the stories about what God has done in your life. These are treasures of redemptive truth and eternal life! As **Isaiah 40:8 says, "The grass withers, the flower fades, but the word of our God stands forever."**

Therefore, pray as a family that God will use you to accomplish His purposes and leave good legacies that will keep your children and family in godliness. With Christ in your life, you can build a legacy for all to see. When we are in Christ, we have a way out of an ungodly heritage, and we are empowered to establish a godly heritage. The Spirit of God enables us to change what we have received and build something different. By following Paul's example, we can help form the Destiny of our great-great-grandchildren. As **Psalm 78:4 says, "We will not hide them from their children, telling the generation to come the praises of the Lord, and His strength and His wonderful works that He has done."**

Obedience to Christ is one step towards leaving a legacy of glory so learn to create a home that honours God. Pass God's commands on to your children and teach them the way to spiritual growth. Be prayerful as a family. Having the presence of Christ helps and guides us to leave a godly legacy in other's lives.

Be firm about your choices and intentions. Make sure that your choices line up with the Word of God because the legacy you leave is the life you lead so it is important to build your life upon the eternal Word of God.

Write and pass on your spiritual, ethical will. Articulate your values, wisdom, and blessings to your loved ones and those who come after you long after you are gone. An ethical will is a way of telling people your personal story, tying together accomplishments, how you lived your life, and what you hope your heirs will take from it. This is your way of still being in the room. A spiritual, ethical will is not a legal will but a record of who you are, a gift to the present and to the future which you offer to your loved ones while you are still alive to express how you want to be remembered after you are gone.

In short, your spiritual, ethical will reminds your descendants who you were, how you lived, and what you contributed to the world. As Jesus said in **Matthew 5:15-16: "Nor do they light a lamp and put it under a basket, but on a lampstand, and it gives light to all who are in the house. Let your light so shine before men, that they may see your good works and glorify your Father in heaven."**

You can leave an enduring legacy in many ways. As **Proverbs 13:22 says, "A good man leaves an inheritance to his children's children, but the wealth of the sinner is stored up for the righteous."** Consider doing the following:

- Teaching and showing your children and grandchildren to know and serve the Lord.

- Living a godly life and teaching by example, remembering **Daniel 12:3: "Those who are wise shall shine like the brightness of the firmament, and those who turn many to righteousness like the stars forever and ever."**

- Basing your life upon the eternal Word of God and teaching others to do the same.

- Winning souls to Christ, remembering **Proverbs 11:30: "The fruit of the righteous is a tree of life, and he who wins souls is wise."**

- Touching the lives of younger people with the wisdom the years have given you, remembering Paul's advice in **Titus 2:3-5: "the older women likewise, that they be reverent in behaviour, not slanderers, not given to much wine, teachers of good things that they admonish the young women to love their husbands, to love their children, to be discreet, chaste, homemakers, good, obedient to their own husbands, that the word of God may not be blasphemed."**

- Make your local church a beacon of truth and a blessing to your community. As it says in **1 Corinthians 12:27-28: "Now you are the body of Christ, and members individually. And God has appointed these in the church: first apostles, second prophets, third teachers, after that miracles, then gifts of healings, helps, administrations, varieties of tongues."**

6. **WHAT ARE THE HINDRANCES AND THREATS TO BUILDING YOUR LEGACY?**

i)   Lack of Focus

This occurs whenever you are not deliberate or intentional in living with your legacy in mind. Your legacy will not create or build itself. Lack of focus leads to lack of preparation which becomes a hindrance to building your legacy. This can lead to leaving our affairs in a mess and forcing others to clean up after us when we are gone. It means we also leave a legacy of pain and suffering when disputes arise among our family members. Failure to leave a will, and lack of thoughtful planning, is the opposite of wisdom. Focus is key. Focus on careful deliberate actions that create your legacy. Do not procrastinate!

ii)   Failure to Achieve our Goals

Maybe we fail to set any goals, or, if we do, we lack sufficient passion, discipline, and willpower to achieve them. Sometimes this can be because we never discover our purpose, calling and Destiny, so we end up living aimlessly.

iii)   Internal Pain

We can fail to build a legacy when we become overwhelmed by past or present traumatic situations which result in feelings of inadequacy, insecurity, and chronic failure, leading to low self-worth and lack of confidence. The fruit of this is ineffectiveness because deep down you think you have no value to pass on to others.

iv)   A Failure to Make Time

If we have a disorganised lifestyle, or we are over-busy, living a cluttered life, our focus will be on being reactive not proactive, thereby causing us to fail to work towards the future, which is one of the prerequisites of legacy building.

v)   Lack of Conviction or Faith

What you believe is a powerful tool. Since building a legacy is not going to be easy - because there will be roadblocks and nothing will go exactly as planned - you must have a strong conviction and unshakable faith that leaving a legacy is crucial and that you have what it takes to build and leave a great legacy. Your beliefs will keep you going. If you don't have such beliefs and convictions, you won't build a legacy.

7.   WHAT ARE THE EFFECTS AND EXAMPLES OF A GOOD, LASTING LEGACY?

A legacy is only a good legacy if it shows evidence of lasting fruit in the lives of those it was intended to touch and benefit. As mentioned in an earlier section, your sphere is where you are ordained to fulfil your purpose and cause a positive impact. This leaves certain footprints that form vital evidence of the goodness of your legacy. Your legacy is how you will be remembered; it is the evidential outcome of a life well lived and a purpose fulfilled.

A legacy includes impact and influence. It also includes significant contributions and accomplishments and a reputation about you that continues to speak long after you have gone. While fulfilling your purpose in your ordained sphere, you must aim to become a living legend and you must thereafter leave a legacy that will bless your generation and future generations for years to come. You must become a history maker in your sphere.

Some of the evidence that you have left positive footprints are the following:

- **Transformed Lives**

Werner Erhard says, "You and I possess within ourselves, at every moment of our lives, under all circumstances, the power to transform the quality of our lives. Knowing that is what the work is about." Your sphere of influence contains people with dilemmas that you have been placed there to solve. As you fulfil your purpose, lives should be positively transformed. Others should be visibly empowered with changed mindsets to fulfil their own purposes and enter their own destinies. Other people's potential must be unleashed to its full and maximum capacity. As Paul wrote in **2 Corinthians 3:18: "But we all, with unveiled face, beholding as in a mirror the glory of the Lord, are being transformed into the same image from glory to glory, just as by the Spirit of the Lord."**

Transforming lives will entail releasing healing, restoration, and restitution. It will include realigning people to their purposes and ushering them from distress to Destiny in all areas of their lives - physical, emotional, mental, intellectual, social, financial, and spiritual. This will result in changed habits and behaviours, leading to a transformed culture.

- **A Voice for the Voiceless**

Stephen Covey says, *"Find your voice and inspire others to find theirs."*

Within your sphere, you must become an opinion shaper and a voice that cannot be ignored. You must be able to shape the culture and the protocols in that sphere for the benefit of the place and the people. Tariq Ramadan says,

"To be courageous is to be a voice for the voiceless."

You must become a voice to the voiceless by speaking for the people who cannot speak for themselves, by speaking out against social ills and evils – for example, by advocating against vices like gross injustice, abuse, discrimination, oppression, against the people at your sphere – and by speaking up and being heard above all the other voices, most of which will be selfish and self-serving, dictatorial and harsh, critical and judgmental, as well as profane and filthy. You must raise your voice of reason, reconciliation, and encouragement above the clamour. Furthermore, you must also speak around your sphere and offer ideas, wisdom, and strategies. You must also speak into situations and make powerful decrees to dispel the toxic atmosphere and create a healthy one.

- **Resurrecting Dead Dreams**

The historian Aberjhani said, "Hearts rebuilt from hope resurrect dreams killed by hate." You must be able to speak words of life to resurrect, rejuvenate, and revive anything good that died because of negative voices and influences. You carry life and resurrection power to your sphere. Remember what Ghandi once taught: *"Every living faith must have within itself the power of rejuvenation if it is to live."*

In your sphere, there will be things that have become dormant and dead out of neglect, mismanagement, fear, hopelessness, oppression, or through the lack of necessary resources to keep them alive. Such things will include gifts and skills, visions and dreams. Your duty is to release resurrection and life. As Goethe once wrote, **"We must always change, renew, rejuvenate ourselves; otherwise, we harden."**

- **Breaking Cycles of Barrenness**

Psalm 113:9 says, **"He grants the barren woman a home, like a joyful mother of children. Praise the Lord."**

You must be able to break every cycle of barrenness, unproductivity, and fruitlessness in your sphere so that people become productive. You must release the right words, actions, impact, influence, and transformational change. The barrenness in your sector or sphere of assignment could include the following:

Physical Barrenness

You may see this in women who cannot have children, or in animals who cannot fulfil their purpose because of sickness.

Ecological Barrenness

This is when there is barrenness in the land. Fields are unproductive for whatever reasons, leading to poverty instead of abundance.

Intellectual Barrenness

This includes fruitless mindsets, evidenced in the absence of new ideas or strategies, leading to organisations lacking the creativity needed to move forward.

Institutional Barrenness

When institutions are unable to birth productivity or profit. Through prayer, teaching, and the rebuilding of people's capacity, you can break cycles of barrenness in all the above.

- **Uprooting Negative Foundations**

Shawn Achor says, **"By changing our mindset and habits, we can actually dramatically change the course of life, improving intelligence, productivity, the quality of our lives and daily outcomes."** You must be able to uproot, destroy, nullify, and render powerless any entrenched negativity in your sphere that has kept people in bondage. Strongholds such as corruption, greed, apartheid, poverty, tribalism, violence, witchcraft, generational cycles and patterns in families and institutions, diseases, must be eradicated for there to be any meaningful change and transformation. Remember what Norman Vincent Peale said, **"Negative thinking definitely attracts negative results."**

- **Planting Positive Foundations**

Someone once said, **"Without a solid foundation, you will have trouble creating anything of value."** After uprooting negativity, you must plant and establish positive foundations to direct and guide the people, including systems and policies to allow growth and transformation. Remember **Jeremiah 1:10: "See, I have this day set you over the nations and over the kingdoms, to root out and to pull down, to destroy and to throw down, to build and to plant."**

You must establish foundations for strong families, churches, and other institutions. You must put in place robust economic strategies, educational platforms, vehicles of justice, truth, and freedom that will uphold right laws and regulations.

- **Improving the Atmosphere**

The atmosphere in your sphere may not be conducive for you to fulfil your purpose and leave positive footprints. This atmosphere is made up of surrounding influences, emotions, feelings, and moods. These may make the prevailing tone oppressive, limiting, hostile, or apathetic. You must symbolically roll away the atmosphere of darkness above the people by virtue of your transformational work on the ground. It is this terrestrial goodness that creates an open heaven under which you have the liberty to enable people to understand who they were born to be and what they were created to do.

Some of the great women who left positive lasting legacies are the following:

Mother Teresa (1910-1997)

An inspirational woman admired by many worldwide, Mother Theresa served as a missionary in Kolkata, India. She worked for the vulnerable and for children at risk through acts of charity and mercy. Here are some of the inspirational things she said:

"Do not wait for leaders; do it alone, person to person."

"God doesn't require us to succeed; he only requires that you try."

"Keep the joy of loving God in your heart and share this joy with all you meet, especially your family."

"Before you speak, it is necessary for you to listen, for God speaks in the silence of the heart."

"Little things are indeed little, but to be faithful in little things is a great thing."

"If we really want to love, we must learn how to forgive."

"Give yourself fully to God. He will use you to accomplish great things on the condition that you believe much more in His love than in your own weakness."

"Speak tenderly... Let there be kindness in your face, in your eyes, in your smile, in the warmth of your greeting. Don't only give your care but give your heart as well."

"Everybody today seems to be in such a terrible rush, anxious for greater developments and greater riches and so on, so that children have very little time for their parents. Parents have very little time for each other and in the home begins the disruption of peace in the world."

"There is a terrible hunger for love. We all experience that in our lives - the pain, the loneliness. We must have the courage to recognize it. The poor you may have right in your own family. Find them. Love them."

"Like Jesus, we belong to the world not living for ourselves but for others. The joy of the Lord is our strength."

Wangari Maathai (1940-2011)

Founder of the Green Belt Movement, Wangari Maathai was honoured worldwide for her work for the environment, democracy, and peace. She left a legacy of campaigning for environmental awareness and she was championed as the best at propagating environmental degradation awareness. She was the first African woman to win the Nobel Peace Prize in 2004. Here are some of her most inspirational comments.

"Human rights are not things that are put on the table for people to enjoy. These are things you fight for and then you protect."

"Today we are faced with a challenge that calls for a shift in our

thinking, so that humanity stops threatening its life-support system. We are called to assist the Earth to heal her wounds and, in the process, heal our own - indeed to embrace the whole of creation in all its diversity, beauty, and wonder. Recognizing that sustainable development, democracy and peace are indivisible is an idea whose time has come."

"I'm very conscious of the fact that you can't do it alone. It's teamwork. When you do it alone you run the risk that when you are no longer there nobody else will do it."

"Education, if it means anything, should not take people away from the land, but instil in them even more respect for it, because educated people are in a position to understand what is being lost. The future of the planet concerns all of us, and all of us should do what we can to protect it. As I told the foresters, and the women, you don't need a diploma to plant a tree."

"There are opportunities even in the most difficult moments."

"The generation that destroys the environment is not the generation that pays the price. That is the problem."

"In trying to explain this linkage, I was inspired by a traditional African tool that has three legs and a basin to sit on. To me the three legs represent three critical pillars of just and stable societies. The first leg stands for democratic space, where rights are respected, whether they are human rights, women's rights, children's rights, or environmental rights. The second represents sustainable and equitable management and resources. And the third stands for cultures of peace that are deliberately cultivated within communities and nations. The basin, or seat, represents society and its prospects for development. Unless all three legs are in place, supporting the seat, no society can thrive. Neither can its citizens develop their skills and creativity. When one leg is missing, the seat is unstable;

when two legs are missing, it is impossible to keep any state alive; and when no legs are available, the state is as good as a failed state. No development can take place in such a state either. Instead, conflict ensues."

"Finally, I was able to see that if I had a contribution I wanted to make, I must do it, despite what others said. That I was OK the way I was. That it was all right to be strong."

"As I swept the last bit of dust, I made a covenant with myself: I will accept. Whatever will be, will be. I have a life to lead. I recalled words a friend had told me, the philosophy of her faith. 'Life is a journey and a struggle,' she had said. 'We cannot control it, but we can make the best of any situation.' I was indeed in quite a situation. It was up to me to make the best of it."

"Throughout my life, I have never stopped to strategize about my next steps. I often just keep walking along, through whichever door opens. I have been on a journey and this journey has never stopped. When the journey is acknowledged and sustained by those I work with, they are a source of inspiration, energy, and encouragement. They are the reasons I kept walking, and will keep walking, as long as my knees hold out."

"A tree has roots in the soil yet reaches to the sky. It tells us that in order to aspire we need to be grounded and that no matter how high we go it is from our roots that we draw sustenance. It is a reminder to all of us who have had success that we cannot forget where we came from. It signifies that no matter how powerful we become in government or how many awards we receive, our power and strength and our ability to reach our goals depend on the people, those whose work remain unseen, who are the soil out of which we grow, the shoulders on which we stand."

"There comes a time when humanity is called to shift to a new level of consciousness . . . that time is now."

"We all share one planet and are one humanity; there is no escaping this reality."

"No matter how dark the cloud, there is always a thin, silver lining, and that is what we must look for. The silver lining will come, if not to us then to the next generation or the generation after that. And maybe with that generation the lining will no longer be thin."

"When we plant trees, we plant the seeds of peace and hope."

"Hallowed landscapes lost their sacredness and were exploited as the local people became insensitive to the destruction, accepting it as a sign of progress."

"The world's interactions with Africa are not necessarily motivated by altruism, but by the self-interest of states seeking to maximize their opportunities and minimize their costs, often at the expense of those who are not in a position to do either."

"What people see as fearlessness is really persistence."

"When we plant trees, we plant the seeds of peace and seeds of hope. We also secure the future for our children."

Maya Angelou (1928-2014)

A celebrated American poet and renowned writer, novelist and filmmaker, Maya Angelou inspired millions with her wisdom and insights. She was awarded the Presidential Medal of Arts Award and received Grammy Awards. She has received over fifty honorary degrees. Her death truly stirred up the souls of many worldwide and her legacy lives on. Here are some inspirational quotes.

"Courage is the most important of all virtues, because without courage, you cannot practice any of the other virtues consistently."

"I have found that among its other benefits, giving liberates the soul of the giver."

"The caged bird sings with a fearful trill

Of things unknown but longed for still,

And his tune is heard on the distant hill

For the caged birds sings of freedom."

"If you don't like something, change it. If you can't change it, change your attitude."

"We may encounter many defeats, but we must not be defeated."

"I've learned that people will forget what you said, people will forget what you did, but people will never forget how you made them feel."

"Words mean more than what is set down on paper. It takes the human voice to infuse them with deeper meaning."

"How important it is for us to recognize and celebrate our heroes and she-roes!"

"To grow up is to stop putting blame on parents."

"We are only as blind as we want to be."

"The intensity with which young people live demands that they 'black out' as often as possible."

"Home is a refuge, not only from my worries, my terrible concerns. I like beautiful things around me. I like them to be beautiful because it delights my eyes and my soul is lifted up."

"You may not control the events that happen to you, but you can decide not to be reduced by them."

"When people show you who they are, believe them the first time."

"Let gratitude be the pillow upon which you kneel to say your nightly prayer. And let faith be the bridge you build to overcome evil and welcome good."

"If you get, give. If you learn, teach."

"In the flush of love's light, we dare to be brave, and suddenly we see that love costs all we are and will ever be. Yet, it is only love which sets us free."

"I believe that each of us comes from the creator trailing wisps of glory."

Ellen Johnson Sirleaf (1936 -)

The first African elected female president and head of state of Liberia, Ellen Johnson Sirleaf was recognized for her efforts in the nonviolent struggle for the safety of women and for women's rights. She was awarded the Nobel Peace Prize in 2011. She is known for her advocacy and for fighting dictators, corruption, and poverty through the empowerment of women and girls. Here are some of her most memorable sayings.

"One has to look at my life story to see what I've done. I've paid a heavy price that many people don't realize."

"I just think that unless you have that cohesiveness in the family unit, the male character tends to become very dominant, repressive and insensitive. So much of this comes also from a lack of education."

"As more men become more educated and women get educated, the value system has to be more enhanced and the respect for human dignity and human life made better."

"When I took office, Liberia began to recover from years of neglect. Our people have brought clean water into the heart of Monrovia to children who have never known water from a tap - efforts are underway to expand water projects as much as possible throughout the country."

"The future belongs to us because we have taken charge of it. We have the commitment, we have the resourcefulness, and we have the strength of our people to share the dream across Africa of clean water for all."

"The people of Liberia know what it means to be deprived of clean water, but we also know what it means to see our children begin to smile again with a restoration of hope and faith in the future."

"Women work harder. And women are more honest; they have less reasons to be corrupt."

"I beg you, I'm no magician. I can't just wave a magic wand."

"Liberia just needs to go through this one political transition and it can really take off. Everything's in place now. We cannot afford to put the country in the hands of someone that lacks the experience."

"I think the majority of the Liberian people want peace."

"All girls know that they can be anything now. That transformation is to me one of the most satisfying things."

"I work hard, I work late, I have nothing on my conscience. When I go to bed, I sleep."

"I underestimated the low level of capacity. I also underestimated the cultural roots of corruption."

"I don't think people understand the awesomeness of the destruction of this country – its institutions, its infrastructure, its law, its morals."

"I stand by it. I take the criticism for it. I think it's unfair, but yes, there is a thing about nepotism, and we all try to respect it."

"I've been involved in politics for quite some time. I've held positions, and my experiences are very deep, and I think I have the capacity, the courage, and the character to institute the kinds of reforms that are so desperately needed."

"In terms of being able to renew my nation, to be able to bring back a devastated country, to restore hope to our people, to lift women and to give them a new horizon, a new ambition and new dreams, in respect of all of that, I think we've accomplished it, and I feel very good about that."

"I would like to make sure, first of all, that our women in the informal sector – I mean, these are the farmers and the traders; many of them are not educated, many of them lacking literacy – have better working conditions. And we've done a lot to be able to achieve that."

"We have to overcome the practice of male domination – even though it's changing, and changing, and changing in Liberia quite drastically."

"My mother was the strength. She was the anchor. She was a preacher and a teacher."

"We've done a lot to restore Liberia's credibility, Liberia's reputation, Liberia's presence."

"I'm not talking about what you hear from 5 percent of the population on the radio, in the papers. I don't pay attention to it. I travel around the country. I'm happy I have a good relationship with the people."

"My mother was a disciplinarian. She believed that when young girls start to go out with young boys, they get married."

"I think we're ready for succession. We just must try to do it right."

"My calling was first of all to ensure there was peace in the country, because we could easily have gone back to war. In the midst of the country, there were still warlords; there were many child soldiers who had never gone to school – they were part of the social setting – compromises had to be made."

Susan B. Anthony (1820-1906)

Awarded the Professional Women's Leadership Award, Susan Anthony advocated for women's suffrage, women's property rights, and the abolition of slavery. She said:

"I do not demand equal pay for any women save those who do equal work in value. Scorn to be coddled by your employers; make them understand that you are in their service as workers, not as women."

"I have given my life and all I am to it, and now I want my last act to be to give it all I have, to the last cent."

"Woman must have a purse of her own, and how can this be, so long as the wife is denied the right to her individual and joint earnings?"

"Here, in the first paragraph of the Declaration, is the assertion of the natural right of all to the ballot; for how can 'the consent of the governed' be given, if the right to vote be denied?"

"I distrust those people who know so well what God wants them to do to their fellows, because it always coincides with their own desires."

"Are you going to cater to the whims and prejudices of people who have no intelligent knowledge of what they condemn?"

"What you should do is to say to outsiders that a Christian has neither more nor less rights in our association than an atheist."

"When our platform becomes too narrow for people of all creeds and of no creeds, I myself shall not stand upon it."

"You would better educate ten women into the practice of liberal principles than to organize a thousand on a platform of intolerance and bigotry."

"It was we, the people, not we, the white male citizens, nor yet we, the male citizens; but we, the whole people, who formed this Union."

"The work of woman is not to lessen the severity or the certainty of the penalty for the violation of the moral law, but to prevent this violation by the removal of the causes which lead to it."

"Whoever controls work and wages, controls morals."

"Oh, if I could but live another century and see the fruition of all the work for women! There is so much yet to be done."

"To think I have had more than 60 years of hard struggle for a little liberty, and then to die without it seems so cruel."

Nadia Murad (1993-still alive)

From Northern Iraq, Nadia Murad was recognized and honoured with the Nobel Peace Prize in 2016 for her advocacy for the survivors of Yazidi genocide and worldwide victims of violence. She fights for the welfare of women and children affected by war and against sexual violence and human trafficking. She said:

"I want to be the last girl in the world with a story like mine."

"I still think that being forced to leave your home out of fear is one of the worst injustices a human being can face."

"You don't know who will open the door next to attack you, just that it will happen, and that tomorrow might be worse."

"Change can happen when one least expects it. I know this to be true because my life changed in an instant."

"I chose to speak because I believed the world needed to know the truth and I wanted justice."

"If we don't speak up today, tomorrow this will continue."

"We need justice. Justice for women. We want people to accept women's messages, so women won't be afraid to talk about what they went through."

"After what happened to me, I realise the most difficult thing is to be a woman."

"Our faith is in our actions. We welcome strangers into our homes, give money and food to those who have none, and sit with the body of a loved one before burial. Even being a good student, or kind to your spouse, is an act equal to prayer. Things that keep us alive and allow poor people to help others, like simple bread, are holy."

"Your past life becomes a distant memory, like a dream. Your body doesn't belong to you, and there's no energy to talk or to fight or to think about the world outside. There is only rape and the numbness that comes with accepting that this is now your life."

"Hopelessness is close to death."

"Deciding to be honest was one of the hardest decisions I have ever made, and also the most important."

"I was freed, but I do not enjoy the feeling of freedom because those who have committed these crimes have not been held accountable."

Kathryn Kuhlman (1907-1976)

Kathryn Kuhlman is remembered for her successful radio and television healing ministry in the USA. Now her spiritual legacy continues to touch lives across the globe. She is a great role model to women in Christian ministry today. She said:

"God is not looking for gold vessels or silver vessels. He is looking for willing vessels."

"Wherever you find real love, you will also find humility. Remember something: humility is not a weak and timid quality. Too often we feel that humility is a sign of weakness. This is not so. It is the sign of strength and security."

"Today, Jesus stands ready to hear your cry and to answer prayer for you. He is interested in every detail of your life. He knows you better than you know yourself."

"Living with faith and courage is something that life requires of each of us. Never, absolutely never, give up! Never give in no matter what! Fight it through! And I promise you something with all of my heart - God will help you."

"Great sea captains are made in rough waters and deep seas."

"The greatest human attainment in all the world is for a life to be so surrendered to Him that the name of God Almighty will be glorified through that life."

"I surrendered unto Him all there was of me; everything! Then for the first time I realized what it meant to have real power."

"God does not patch up the old life or make certain repairs on the old life; He gives a new life, through the new birth."

"The only limit to the power of Almighty God lies within you and me."

"Faith is that quality or power by which the things desired become the things possessed."

"Whether life grinds a man down or polishes him depends on what he's made of."

"I didn't have any looks, I didn't have any talent, and it was easy for me to say to the Lord, 'I don't have anything.' If you only knew where I came from ... this leetle-bitty town with no more than twelve hundred people in it. So ... anything I am today, He is the one who has done it [ellipses in source]."

"When Jesus died on the cross and cried out, 'It is finished!' He not only died for our sins, but for our diseases too."

"Any truth, no matter how valid, if emphasized to the exclusion of other truths of equal importance, is practical error."

"A little knowledge and an over-abundance of zeal always tends to be harmful. In the area involving religious truths, it can be disastrous."

Rosa Parks (1913-2005)

We remember Rosa Parks as a dynamic gamechanger. She was an American activist in the civil rights movement best known for her pivotal role in the Montgomery bus boycott. The United States Congress has called her "the first lady of civil rights" and "the mother of the freedom movement." Parks' act of defiance and the Montgomery bus boycott became important symbols of the movement. She became an international icon of resistance to racial segregation. She organized and collaborated with civil rights leaders, including Edgar Nixon, president of the local chapter of the NAACP, and Martin Luther King Jr. She said:

"Whatever my individual desire was to be free, I was not alone. There were many others who felt the same way."

"People always say that I didn't give up my seat because I was tired, but that isn't true…No, the only tired I was, was tired of giving in."

"I have learnt over the years that when one's mind is made up, knowing what must be done does away with fear."

Funmilayo Ransome-Kuti (1900-1978)

A Nigerian educator, political campaigner, suffragist, and women's rights activist, Ransome-Kuti established the Abeokuta Women's Union and fought for women's rights, demanding better representation of women in local governing bodies and an end to unfair taxes on market women. Ransome-Kuti received the Lenin Peace Prize and was awarded membership in the Order of the Niger for her work. She said:

"As for the charges against me, I am unconcerned, I am beyond their timid lying morality, and so I am beyond caring."

"The heart of a woman can change the world."

Emmeline Pankhurst (1858-1928)

Emmeline Pankhurst was a founding member of a group of women called the Suffragettes, who fought hard to win women the right to vote in the UK. They often used violent and extreme tactics to do this, and Emmeline was no stranger to a prison cell as a result. When World War One broke out, however, she recognized that she should help with the war effort, and she encouraged other Suffragettes to do the same. While the men were away, many women like Emmeline took on jobs that men traditionally did. The women earned lots of respect doing this and it showed just how much women contributed to society and, therefore, how much they deserved the right to vote. In 1918, a law was passed which allowed certain women the right to vote. She said:

"I would rather be a rebel than a slave."

"You must make women count as much as men; you must have an equal standard of morals; and the only way to enforce that is through giving women political power so that you can get that equal moral standard registered in the laws of the country. It is the only way."

"Better that we should die fighting than be outraged and dishonoured... Better to die than to live in slavery"

"We women suffragists have a great mission – the greatest mission the world has ever known. It is to free half the human race, and through that freedom to save the rest."

From the Bible we find the following women who also left positive lasting legacies:

Naomi (Ruth's mother-in-law)

Naomi is a good role model as a mentor and a Destiny connector. She is found in the *Book of Ruth*. As Ruth's mother-in-law, she was instrumental in ushering Ruth to her Destiny, even as she entered her own.

Deborah

Deborah was a woman leader in the *Book of Judges*. We celebrate her as a great role model for women leaders today. She arose as a zealous leader to fight against oppression when most people, including men, cowered in fear.

Queen Esther

We remember Queen Esther for her resilience, tenacity, and wisdom when she devised a spectacular strategy to change the king's mind from annihilating her people as she outmanoeuvred the schemes of the wicked.

Unfortunately, there are some other women from the Bible and from history who left a negative legacy:

Jezebel

We remember Jezebel as a wicked woman dedicated to the destruction of leaders. Today, she is synonymous with a negative spirit of control, manipulation, and witchcraft.

Potiphar's Wife

We find Potiphar's wife in the *Book of Genesis*. We remember Potiphar's wife as one who sought to derail Joseph and she went on to falsely accuse him of immorality. The idiom "Potiphar's wife" today signifies a character that seeks to destroy righteous men.

Delilah

We find Delilah in the *Book of Judges* as a weak woman who was easily manipulated by her wicked people to derail and deceive the man of God (Samson) from his calling and purpose.

Irma Grese (1923-1945)

An SS guard at the Nazi concentration camps of Ravensbrück and Auschwitz, Grese served as warden of the women's section of Bergen-Belsen. She was convicted of crimes involving the ill-treatment and murder of prisoners committed at Auschwitz and Bergen-Belsen concentration camps and sentenced to death at the Belsen trial. Executed at 22 years of age, Grese was the youngest woman to die judicially under British law in the 20th century.

Maesaiah Thabane

Another woman to leave a negative legacy, Thabane was the first lady of Lesotho, a small kingdom surrounded entirely by South Africa. She was charged with murdering her ex-husband just two days before his inauguration in June 2017. She was also charged with the attempted murder of a second woman who was with the former first lady the night she was killed.

Sarah Jo Pender (1979-still alive)

This woman has left a legacy of notoriety. She is an American woman convicted along with her former boyfriend, Richard Edward Hull, of murdering their roommates - Andrew Cataldi and Tricia Nordman - on October 24, 2000, in Indiana. She came to national attention in August 2008 after she escaped from the Rockville Correctional Facility and was featured on America's Most Wanted. She was recaptured by police in December at a house in Chicago.

Destiny Questions To Ponder On

1. *How else would you interpret and define a legacy?*

2. *What other reasons do you think there are for you to leave a legacy?*

3. *Beyond your children, family, society and nation who else do you believe stands to benefit most from your legacy?*

4. *What are the other bricks that you would consider necessary in building your legacy?*

5. *What in your opinion is the most important type of legacy for you to leave?*

6. *What are the greatest hindrances and threats that you have personally encountered in your attempts to build your legacy?*

7. *Name at least 3 women who left a lasting legacy that has benefited you personally?*

Chapter 10

A WOMAN'S DEFINING DECADE'S

Understanding The Factors That Define Your Identity At Every Age

Chapter Preview

1. **Your Trendy Twenties**

    A decade characterized by your friends, fashion fads, flames and fathers

2. **Your Thriving Thirties**

    A decade characterized by your career, children and candid choices

3. **Your Formidable Forties**

    A decade characterized by your strength, spontaneity and selectiveness

4. **Your Feisty Fifties**

    A decade characterized by your milestones, missed miles, mid-life crisis and masterfulness

5. **Your Sensational Sixties**

    A decade characterized by your groundedness, generosity and graciousness

6. **Your Serene Seventies**

    A decade characterized by your significance, sagacity and supremacy

7. **Your Elegant Eighties**

    A decade which defines you as a living legend, a leading lady and a luminary

OPENING REMARKS

As a woman of destiny, and as you transition from one decade of your life to another, it will be necessary for you to examine each decade and ascertain the factors that sought or seek to define you in that decade for purposes of deciding which of those factors should have defined you or should define you, and those that should not or should not have defined you.

Thereafter, your task is to purpose that even though you may not have consciously decided what you would allow to define you, in each of your decades (that have now passed) you will nonetheless ensure that going forward, you will consciously take charge and authority over what you'll allow to define you in your remaining decades.

Suffice to say that every woman should get a revelation that her Purpose and Calling and the Destiny she was called to fulfil defines her in every decade of her life.

In this section, we are looking at factors from various decades of a woman's life that most likely define her.

Ensuring that you are defined by the right factors in each decade of your life will definitely impact on your ability to fulfil your purpose and enter your destiny.

Perhaps the most relevant decades in a woman's life in terms of those that affect her self-identity, are from her twenties to her eighties. Prior to her twenties (while she is in her teens and pre-teens) she is not really in control of her decisions because she is either under parental control or guardianship care. After her eighties (when she enters her noble nineties) she is also not really in control and she is also most likely under the care of her loved ones who then make her decisions for her.

So as a woman who is serious and passionate about fulfilling your purpose (and destiny and knowing that your identity is crucial to your ability in fulfilling that purpose and destiny) then it is paramount that you pay attention to what factors in each of your decades, you will allow to define you and those that you will not allow to define you. This way you can dance through your decades without losing or distorting the core of your identity, and grow stronger and more secure in who you are as you move from one decade to another.

Feedback from several women who are at various decades of their lives, has revealed that generally, and commonly, there are at certain factors that seek to define most (even though not all) women in their various decades.

For example, a woman in her **twenties**, will mostly be defined by certain F's namely: Her Friends, Fashion fads, Flames and her Fathers…

And in her **thirties**, by certain C's namely: her Career, her Children and her Choices.

… in her **forties** by certain S's namely: her Strength, her Spontaneity and Selectiveness.

in her **fifties** by certain M's namely: her Milestones, Missed miles, her Midlife crisis, and her Masterfulness.

in her **sixties** by certain G's namely: her Groundedness, her Generosity and Graciousness

in her **seventies** by certain S's namely: her Significance, her Sagacity and her Supremacy.

and in her **eighties** by certain L's namely: as a Living Legend, as a Leading Lady and as a Liberating Light.

This does not mean that these factors are the right ones that should have defined her, or that should define her when she reaches that decade, it is simply a reflection on what most women who have already passed these decade say, sought to define them.

As to what should or should not define you in each decade is a personal choice, so the purpose here is to simply provoke you to be very intentional in choosing what should define you, as you dance through the decades of your life

1. YOUR TRENDY TWENTIES

A Decade Characterized by Your Friends, Fashion Fads, Flames and Fathers

"Your 20's are your selfish years. Old enough to make the right decisions and young enough to make the wrong ones. Be selfish with your time- travel, explore, fall in and out of love, be ridiculous and silly, stupid and wild. Be 20something." ~ Unknown

In terms of Calling and Destiny chances are you may not yet have discovered your Purpose and Calling, but as you progress to the mid and the end of this decade you will become more aware of your gifts, talents, skills and competence sufficiently enough to start taking responsibility for discovering and embarking on that which you were born and created for.

This is an age of transitioning from girlhood to woman hood. It is often said that the number twenty symbolizes or represents a period of waiting to grow into another level or a period of waiting to get something that you were not previously ready for.

In your trendy 20's there are some F's that seek to define you namely: your friends, flames, fashion fads, and father figures.

It is in your twenties that you may begin to find your true identity by seeking individuality from your friends but it is usually a difficult uphill task because you are still young and impressionable.

Even though you are now able to make healthier decisions than you did in your teens, you are nonetheless still not yet experienced enough to process the seriousness and consequences of some of your decisions.

You are definitely more comfortable around your parents and other adult authorities like teachers etc. than you were in your teens. You are less opposed and less suspicious of them as you adamantly continue to seek your independence and freedom, even though often, you are not so ready to accept the responsibility that comes with that freedom and independence that you are asking for.

Paradoxically in your twenties, you appear to prefer being in a crowd socially than being alone. Yet when it comes to working on projects and assignments or even business ideas you may appear to prefer to go it alone, probably because in your twenties you are quite opinionated in wanting to have your own way and you may find it difficult to embrace others people's views and ideas.

Another paradox is that some women in their twenties are very vocal and loudly visible, extremely rebellious, radical, anti-authority and anti-establishment, due to various factors. Some others are extremely self-conscious, always thinking that people are judging them and so they try to fade in the background.

It is worthy of note that those women in their twenties today whether they be born again and very committed to church activities or out there in the world doing worldly things, they are all somehow obsessed with something. (Whether it be social media instead being interested in structured conversations or reading). Unfortunately, many are not yet mature enough to use things like social media, responsibly. They appear naïve as to the adverse long-term effects that social media can have if used irresponsibly because of the consequences that will come to haunt her later.

The number "**two**" symbolizes agreement or covenant, meaning that during this decade, you may sincerely believe in making pacts and binding promises with your friends, flames or fathers and that you take so seriously and when such promises are breached it affects you so deeply and so irreparably for years to come.

i) Your Friends and Fashion Fads

"There are friends, there is family, and then there are friends that become family." ~ Unknown

For most women their girlfriends are very important during their 20's. It will predominantly be like-minded girls who share the same values, same opinions, same fashion trends etc.

Even though in your 20's you may not be as easily influenced and obsessed with your friends as you were in your teens, none the less there is still some strong measure of influence upon one another, no matter how hard you may try to claim your independence.

In other words, the type of **friends** you have in your 20's have a tendency to define who you are to a certain extent.

"True friends are like diamond - bright, beautiful, valuable and always in style." ~ Nicole Richie

In your 20s many young women often give more priority to their friendships than to their families and this can cause a lot of conflicts.

There is obviously peer pressure during this decade because you and your friends are bonded by common values and beliefs. You may find yourself adopting and ascribing to things you have not given much thought to just because your friends are doing it.

And you may find yourself dressing like your friends irrespective of whether what suits your friends suits you. This is because being accepted by your friends is crucial at this stage, and fitting in is key.

"Fashion is instant language." ~ Miuccia Prada

As you move from your early and mid-twenties towards the end of your twenties, there is usually a lot of emotional drama. There is a lot of falling away between friends (who were not really friends) because you were bonded by very fickle and easily breakable interests, so you begin to sieve and sift and remain with those who are real.

Fashion, makeup, body size are extremely crucial at this stage. This is the reason most women in their twenties succumb to dysfunctions such as bulimia and anorexia nervosa seeking to change their body size, including other equally destructive habits like body mutilation etc.

Fortunately, as a woman matures towards the end of her twenties, she begins to view all these things from a different perspective and she starts developing her independent mind her own fashion sense, her style and individuality.

"Fashion is a trend; style is within a person." ~Oscar De la Renta

ii)   Your Flames

"Love is a flame to burn out human wills, Love is a flame to set the will on fire, Love is a flame to cheat men into mire." ~ John Masefield

Your first real romantic fantasy and encounter will probably happen in your 20's where it is more than a high school crush or a flirtation. You are now are a bit more mature transitioning into womanhood and chances are you will experience your first real heart break very intensely and it may have long term effects if you do not manage it.

"Leave an old flame in the past. It will just get worse if you rekindle it" ~Yeong-hun Kim

The reason that the pain can be so intense and take long to heal from, is because you are still young emotionally and therefore not well able to process pain, betrayal etc. like an older woman would.

It is also interesting to note that women at this age whether deeply involved in church or out there in the world are all obsessed about boyfriends. The church girl and Worldly girl's understanding of what a boyfriend relationship may entail, will obviously differ because of the different values, but suffice when it comes to loving and hurting the intensity is the same, whether she is a church girl or not.

Many women in this decade may end up having a boyfriend not because they really want one, but because it is what is expected of them. Since they want to be like their friends and do not want to stand out as if they are a reject or a weirdo. This is considering that at this stage, being liked and admired, approved of and affirmed is very important to a woman in terms of building or eroding her confidence.

Some women may end up marrying a first flame who they encounter in their 20's but it is also noticeable that the earlier in your 20's you marry the higher the chances of a divorce later on (according to what women who married their first flame in their twenties say).

"Never let an old flame burn you again" ~ Unknown

iii)   Your Father's (and Father Figures)

"Behind any great daughter is a truly amazing dad." By Unknown

In your 20's most women will either have a "**present**" and available father or an "**absentee**" father (whether he is deceased, divorced or unknown) and a young woman will therefore be affected differently depending on which scenario she is dealing with.

In the first scenario where the father is **present** and she is a daddy's girl, loved and cherished (and irrespective of whether she is brought up in wealth or poverty) the most important thing for this girl that really boosts and builds her confidence and self-esteem (and which may ultimately define her identity), is her father's attention, approval and affirmation.

"She did not stand alone, but what stood behind her. The most potent force in her life was the dove of her father." ~ Harper Lee

"When I am at my best, I am my father's daughter" ~ Unknown

Sometimes that same attention, approval and affirmation which she enjoyed when younger may become a snare when her father begins to control her decisions and choices, (especially as regards boyfriends). It is at this point the relationship between a daddy's girl and her father may turn sour because she feels suffocated and disheartened by her father's irrational disapproval of any man she may love and present to him. She may even end up marrying someone totally unsuitable for her out of rebellion.

So, for some women, they will be defined by their father's acceptance opinion and approval while others will rebel against it, and refuse to be defined by it.

"No matter how old you get, the hole in your heart created by your father's absence still aches" Unknown

At the other extreme is a woman who grows up with an **absentee father,** whether deceased, divorced or unknown. Some young women may get deeply affected by this and develop a **father wound** that may ultimately shape her identity.

Perhaps the scenario that may affect a young woman at this stage, most severely, is where the father is available to have a relationship with her, but he chooses not to for whatever reasons. This only goes to reinforce the rejection, low self-value, that may ultimately lead this woman to replace her **absent father** with a boyfriend old enough to be her father, (who will provide the material gifts, attention, approval and affirmation that her father failed to give). Naturally many young women may live to regret this choice which was not rationalized, but made as a rebound and from a place of pain, rejection and confusion.

Other effects of this kind of scenario may be self-destructive patterns of behavior, such as substance abuse or early pregnancies etc.

This means that your father whether present or absent and should not have the power to define you during this decade whether positively or negatively, because that approval or rejection may change any time.

Another consequence of an **absentee father** or a father who neglected his daughter, is to make young women unable to form any meaningful romantic relationships because she has lost trust in all men.

"I was never a 'daddy's little girl' or 'daddy's little princess' so when a guy tries to show me some type of affection, I don't know how to react and I end up pushing it." ~Unknown

So, for those still in their 20's reading this book you must decide whether you will allow these F's to define you or whether you will begin to authenticate your own identity by your personal values and beliefs and more importantly by who God says you are.

"On the darkest days, when I feel inadequate, unloved and unworthy, I remember whose daughter I am and I strengthen my crown" ~ Unknown

Advise for Women in Their Trendy Twenties

For those who have passed their trendy twenties, you may have some very valuable advice for those be are still in their trendy twenties which may go something like this:

- Make a concerted effort to understand the power that your true identity has in shaping your destiny which means seeking to understand what should and what should not define you. Desire to know as much about yourself as possible, acknowledge and appreciate your strengths and call out your weaknesses as opposed to denying them, so that you get to know yourself without judging yourself and then change what needs changing for the better and accept yourself and love who you are before you can seek other people to love you.

- Knowing, accepting and loving who you are, **firstly,** stops other people from seeking to define you wrongly or from manipulating you with their love and hate and,

- **secondly** it, leads you to knowing what you want and what you do not want.

- Knowing what you want and what you do not want, especially will stop other people from projecting their likes and dislikes on you or misusing you for their own agendas.

- It will help you to say no respectfully and with courtesy, but without fear so you avoid falling into abuse because you are too fearful and obliging. Try and understand and appreciate your uniqueness early enough, your capacity and abilities so that you do not have to compare or compete with others.

- Get a revelation that you do not have it all by virtue of the basic logic, that you have not lived long enough, so you do not have much experience. So be willing and even eager to accept genuine correction guidance, rebukes, advice, good and wise counsel plus mentorship.

- Beware of your youthful indiscretions because your reputation is priceless and one careless mistake especially in public or on social media can damage your reputation and live to haunt you for many years to come.

- Realize that growing up without a father should actually make you stronger and stop believing that something is lacking in you because your father wasn't there.

- Know your limitations as regards your resources, influence and networks and do not try to live like a woman in her thirties or forties, when you do not have the resources, capacity or the maturity to sustain their kind of lifestyle.

2. YOUR THRIVING THIRTIES

A decade characterized by your career, children and candid choices

By this decade a woman ought to have made some discovery as to her Purpose and Calling especially since her identity is more or less in place. By this age often it is a question of how to balance the fulfilling of her Purpose and Calling with the roles in her life.

This is an age of vigorous, rapid growth and stretching.

The number "**thirty**" and in particular the age of thirty is known as the age of maturity when you are ready to take up certain responsibilities that you were not capable of before this age, like marriage, inheritance and other such responsibilities.

Your 30's are your prime time professionally, physically and emotionally. Someone once said that "**thirty is an attitude**".

"Thirty is your attitude; it says you know what you are doing and you got what it takes to get where you are doing. The fact is you've never been better or smarter or more ready for adventure than you are right now. So welcome to prime time." Unknown

The fact is that you have never been better, smarter or more ready than you are when you are in your thirties. In your thirties you are now taken more seriously than you were in your twenties.

You finally realize the need to get rid of the skinny tight jeans that were a must in your twenties as you begin to dress more comfortably but still stylish and you still look good. Your need for people's opinions and approval on your looks is decreasing, even though you are still proactive in keeping up with fashion trends.

You become less judgmental of others because you have gone through some measure of hell that has made you stronger and more sensitive and tolerant to the suffering of others.

Instead of being critical and judgmental towards others, you develop a better sense of good judgment and discernment.

"Good judgment comes from experience and a lot of that comes from bad judgment." ~ Will Rogers

As a parent in your thirties, you begin to see your parents in you, their habits, behaviors etc. and your relationship with them improves tremendously as you begin to appreciate what they went through in parenting you. You acquire a new respect for them. You begin to appreciate the valuable lessons they taught you and the timeless principles they instilled in you, which did not seem so crucial then but which have now become your foundation in every area of your life.

In your Thriving Thirties, you still have the capacity to dream without fear. It is often said young ones are slaves to dreams, the old are servants to regrets. So, at thirty you need to dream and actualize your dreams to avoid becoming a servant of regret.

In your thirties you begin to whittle down, your circle of friends, so that your true friends crystalize into a smaller core circle as you become aligned and attuned to your true identity. You begin to understand who is and who is not good for you. You also become less dependent on friendships than you were in your 20" s as you begin to take responsibility for your own choices, decisions, happiness or unhappiness (without seeking to blame others or wait on them to live your life for you).

There are three C's that seek to define a woman during this decade, and it is her responsibility to decide, whether they should or should not define her.

i)   Your Career

Your vocation or occupation whether a profession, career or a job, begins to take center stage in your life at this age and you begin to be identified with what you do.

For many women it becomes important to them, that they are taken seriously as regards their career and vocation which means that they become equally self-conscious when they have not yet locked into a career or vocation to be identified with.

Many may even lose confidence where it is taking long to lock into their career choice or a serious stable vocation befitting their level of qualification and desire.

Many women during this stage want stability and to earn well, and it is a time when you are energetic and eager to prove yourself in terms of skills and competence, and how fast you are climbing the success ladder in whatever vocation you are in.

It is during this decade that you have a chance to set a clear career path, and set clear career goals, which will make all the difference in the next decades in determining your success or lack thereof.

In fact, most women say that their Careers, Professions and vocations definitely sought to define them during their thirties, despite the fact a career, profession or vocation. Should not really define your true identity.

ii)   Children

It is also a decade when most women get married and have children or have a child as a single mother. So, marriage and children become new factors that seek to define you depending on how you present and position yourself.

It is truly a decade where you have to grow up and mature overnight because of the diverse crisis, tough times, emotional upheavals, some life-threatening situations like the loss of a child, marital conflicts or the break-up of a marriage, career confusion etc. Apart from having to balance your career and family, you are also having to balance your emotions.

It is during this decade that many women develop a tenacity because they realize that there is no stepping back from these situations, no falling back on parents to savage her. She must confront and deal with all these issues and not only survive them but also thrive through it all.

For those women who may become consumed with their marital status and lose themselves in it, then their identity may become seriously eroded as she becomes "Mrs. So and So". For those who become consumed with their children, to the exclusion of everything else, their identity may become also eroded or erased and she becomes defined as "Mama So and So". This of course leads to an identity crisis, especially where the marriage breaks or the children grow up and leave the nest and she must find herself again.

iii)   Choices

The above two dynamics of career and children obviously means that a woman during this decade, will have some serious life and destiny choices to make, which may build or break her going forward.

So, she must be very alert and very deliberate in making those choices, because the choices she makes will define her for a very long time.

The sensitivity of the choices should not be underestimated, considering that they are choices affecting the lives of others, such as children and spouses etc. not just affecting her own life.

Choices, such as, whether to walk out or stay in a dysfunctional marriage, whether to work full time or be a stay home mum, whether to take certain career moves that may be very lucrative but may prejudice her family, what friends and networks she can trust around her, what investments to make.

More importantly streamlining her values and beliefs including salvation and church involvement which are all fundamental choices that have long term effects.

"Your choices whether good or bad define you." ~ Unknown

A woman's choice as to how to balance her career, ambitions and family during this decade, is crucial.

The tendency is to want overnight success so she runs at a speed and takes on so much at the workplace that if she is not careful, she will crush and burn, and neglect her marriage and children.

Advise Women in their Thriving Thirties

- Understand and establish balance in your life so that you do not forsake or neglect your Calling and Destiny because of any one role in your life.
- Take time to solidify good women friends, real genuine friendships, whether socially, professionally or spiritually who will stand with you and have your back during this critical decade.
- Remain positive through every circumstance, build a radical faith, remember the buck will often end with you and there some balls you cannot afford to drop.
- Accept that things will go crazy so that you manage your expectations, learn to deal with the unexpected with a level head lest you drown (because you cannot control human beings such as your children and spouse).
- Be assured that it is okay if you are not married, and have no children during this decade and even if your career has not fallen into place avoid comparing yourself and feeling behind schedule because that may lead you to settle for less than you are entitled to or worth in terms of career and relationship.

3. YOUR FORMIDABLE FORTIES

A Decade Characterized by Strength, Spontaneity and Selectiveness

"At the age of 20 we don't care what the world is thinking of us. At 30s we worry what it is thinking of us. At 40 we discover it wasn't thinking of us at all." Unknown

At this stage most women already have a fortified career or business and they are also deep in the fulfilling of their Purpose and Calling.

This is an age of fortitude and formation, in a strong independent woman, because by now, life has dealt you whatever hand, and you have played both the good and bad and come cut a winner even if it is with some battle scars.

The number 40 symbolizes a season of testing and making. Like a 40 day fast, or 40 weeks of pregnancy formation. So, the number forty is commonly associated with having being judged, tried and tested.

"I love my age, old enough to know better. Young enough not to care, experienced enough to do it right."Angela Bassett

The word **"Formidable"** refers to inspiring awe and respect, one who is powerful and intense, capable and able to overcome challenges and not easily intimidated. It is often said that in your 40's you are old enough to discern and distinguish, so that you can be trusted.

In your 40's it is assumed that you should have arrived and succeeded in whatever you had set out to do, but it is not always the case.

During this decade a woman begins to sincerely love and accept herself and become more authentic, feeding her soul with what she is passionate about. She embraces her real purpose and she commits to it. It is a stage where she builds strong supportive networks professionally and socially beyond her close friend's circle and she becomes allergic to fake friendships, and can easily discern users and abusers around and guards herself against them.

She finally learns the power of saying no, and she categorically refuses to carry other people's monkeys, or allow them to manipulate or control her.

Fashion wise you are no longer defined by size, you let go of any unbearable tight clothing, and you dress appropriately for your age, as you are now comfortable with your body and self-image.

More importantly during this decade you have no unrealistic expectations, there is no acting like you have it all together, you are as real as they come. You desire fulfilling value-based relationships (whether romantically, socially, professionally, spiritually etc.) that are productive, fruitful and aligned to your dreams and goals.

You are a veritable fount of wisdom on diverse issues intellectually, socially, professionally and otherwise and at this stage you may be known as an expert in some area or industry, but you are still ready to train for something else, as you now have more time on your hands.

Many women at this age seek to correct their course where they feel they may have veered off course, and some even seek to make amends for any wrongs with family, friends, colleagues etc. as it dawns upon them that whatever issues they might have had, were never that serious.

During your 40's three S's may seek to define you: -

i)   **Your Strength**

By your forties the storms of life have left you with an inbuilt fortitude and you have become strong mentally, emotionally and professionally and even spiritually. Your strength is visible and causes positive impact wherever your trend.

Your stamina and saying power are undeniable and this often ushers you to sit on serious Boards, Commissions and Trusts etc. and you may experience a significant boost in your career, and profile.

"Success depends upon staying power. The reason for failure in most cases is lack of perseverance." By J.R. Miller

However, this is also the age where some life changing events many take place like financial collapse parenting crisis, divorce etc. and you will need all your strength, failing which you could easily crumple and allow the ugly pain of such traumatic events to cripple you for life. This is where your ability to remain formidable comes in handy.

ii)   **Your Spontaneity**

"Only in spontaneity can we be who we truly are." **By John McLaughlin**

At this stage you are more confident in making sound judgments, decisions and choices so you are more spontaneous and confident in handling issues, and you have a higher risk appetite.

Also, you understand that moments and opportunities must be seized and you cannot afford to be unsure or doubtful or hesitant, so your moves are fast and deliberate.

You have an open natural uninhibited manner, without any constraints because you are now more mature and have more experience to step into situations without over analyzing them.

"The best times are usually random, unplanned and completely spontaneous." Unknown

You also have more enthusiasm and energy in your endeavors and ventures without being reckless or negligent. You have a self-trust, a self- assurance, more opinionated and strong-minded and less procrastinating and definitely more secure in your identity.

"The way that I live my life is on spontaneity." By Melanie Brown

iii)   **Selectiveness**

"As we grow up, we realize it is less important to have lots of friends and more important to have real ones." **By Amanda McRae**

It is a lot harder to get someone out of your life than it is to let them in. So, the more selective you are the smarter you are. In your 40's you have seen and gone through enough, so that you are now more discriminate and selective of your investments, choices, actions, relationships etc.

At this stage your power to be selective will be stronger, because you have enough experience to know what you want and what you do not want (because of some losses you may have suffered). You now know better and you are selective as regards opportunities and positions offered to you, plus at this stage you also know that you are marketable and in demand and you do not have to settle for just anything.

You are of course selective in your relationships and romantic choices, "having been there, done that and bought the T-shirt". In short you are less gullible and less impressionable.

"The older I get the more selective I am in who is in my tribe... I would rather have 4 quarters than a hundred pennies." ~ Unknown

Advise to Women in Their Formidable Forties

- Your focus on destiny in terms of fulfilling your purpose and calling should become stronger at this stage especially since your career, profession or business is probably already solid on its own without too much attention from you.

- You can now slow down, soften your stance, accept help, and eat what you like without apology, but in moderation, allow yourself to be loved by those who genuinely want to love you, without being overly suspicious because you are now mature enough to know what is real and what is fake.

- Your eyesight may start going, symbolizing a dimming in your vision, goals and dreams so you must be careful to ensure you remain sharp.

- You may begin to see the first signs of weariness to remind you of the effects from the storms of life that you have survived, and you may see the first signs of grey hair, symbolizing you've stepped into the wisdom zone.

- Be good to yourself, spend money on self-care, your health, travel, luxury items etc. and spend more times with your parents because at this point, they are transitioning out and it's crucial that you be there.

4. YOUR FEISTY FIFTIES

A Decade Characterized by Your Milestones, Missed Miles, Midlife Crisis and Masterfulness

At this point you are not only credible in your career profession or business; you are also credible in terms of your purpose and calling. It is very clear to all those around you as to what you were called to do even where you may not be doing it to the extent that you should be.

A **feisty woman** is one who is high spirited, gutsy, ballsy determined and courageous full of energy. Some may even call her bossy or aggressive or difficult.

Most women in their 50's are no-nonsense and more focused than ever, knowing that every year now counts.

This is the golden girl age full of favour and grace for many women.

In your 50's you are now moving from seeking success towards seeking significance. It is more about making an impact as opposed to proving yourself and how successful you are.

In your 50's you realize you are more than half way to the end of your life and there might be a tendency to panic, as you take stock and wonder whether you have really accomplished anything worthwhile.

In your 50's you are no longer desperate for romance nor are you clingy and you are sincerely and totally over your ex-relationships (whether they are spouses, boyfriends or girlfriends) and can even relate with them very amicably with no bitterness or woundedness. You definitely know what you want and you communicate your intentions articulately. You are suddenly very conscious of the need to take care of yourself and you are in tune with your age and your biological clock, meaning that, you know that you are not so young anymore and you have no problem with it.

You have had your share of unhappy times and so by your 50's you know you have to be intentional in creating your own happiness so you also intentionally remove yourself from any negative environment.

So, you are very deliberate in shutting out all negative narratives and conversations, which is evident of someone who is in control of her environment and space.

In your 50's it is about quality not quantity so you may begin to downsize and you develop a deeper sense of self-acceptance and a heightened sense of self-esteem. You have better relationships with your children and female friendships. Your time with them is now more structured and organized (by design not by default) and it is clear you now place much more value and time into these relationships.

You take every opportunity to change aspects of your life that you are unhappy about e.g., relationships, health and activities. You sense the hope of new beginnings and new horizons because your 50's can also be a season of transition and new opportunities.

If you have not grown up at 50, you don't have to. This is the golden girl age when you can get away with anything by virtue of the fact that you have already come so far.

3 M's seek to define you is your 50's namely your Milestones or, missed opportunities, your mid-life crisis, your masterfulness.

i)   Your Milestones or Missed Miles

"Remember to celebrate milestones as you prepare for the road ahead." ~ Nelson Mandela

In your 50's it is expected that you will celebrate your "Golden birthday bash" with a bang which will bring you out into the limelight for people to either jubilantly celebrate your milestones or savagely and viciously criticize your missed miles as they measure your success or lack thereof. So, it is crucial you have your own definition of what you consider success to be or else people's opinions may throw you into a serious identity crisis.

At this point you may be tempted to compare yourself with high achievers your age, by what they have accomplished in their fields and you fail to realize that you were running your own race in your own lane, and doing what you were each ordained to do, so you cannot compare your results.

You may also be tempted to compare yourself by using the world's standard of what makes one successful e.g., career and wealth and accomplishments and you fail to look at other significant areas that the world may not see, like family, your impact and influence in transforming lives in society etc.

So, whether it be milestones or missed miles, neither should define you as they do not go to the core of who you really are.

"In life there are milestones each rare and so sweet, sharing with loved ones makes them complete." ~Unknown

ii)   Your Mid-life Crisis

"The truth is out! Mid-life crisis is really a mid-life transformation."
~ Unknown

Your 50's is a season of transition, namely, transition of identity. You may experience a midlife crisis which comes with feelings of regret, guilt, anxiety, loss of self-confidence, dissatisfaction with life, hopelessness, worthlessness.

You may also experience an empty nest syndrome when your grown-up children leave home which comes with feelings of sadness, loss and worry. You must endeavor to overcome your mid-life crisis without allowing it to define you.

How you handle your mid-life crisis will determine how fruitful or fruitless this decade will be for you.

"I think mid-life crisis is just a point where people's careers have reached some plateaus and they have to reflect on their personal relationships." ~ Bill Murray

Being aware in advance that a mid-life crisis comes around this decade will help you to prepare for it and manage it well.

iii)   Your Masterfulness

"You have invited, attracted, created every experience in your life. You are a master creator." ~ Unknown

In your 50's you have definitely mastered many things and you have an undeniable measure of expertise and skills, you are accomplished, artful, adept, experienced, provisioned and well versed in a diverse myriad of issues that have made you the seasoned woman that you are.

Society is not ready to write you off just yet, and you have a whole decade and more before retirement from the formal job market. So, this is your golden age and you are as valuable as gold to many of those around you, so agree and allow yourself to be celebrated and to celebrate yourself without apology.

Advise to Women in Their Feisty Fifties

- Do not allow there to be any doubt in the eyes of those around you as to what your Purpose and Calling is and more importantly that you are fulfilling it faithfully

- Be fully present, appreciate the valuable things in life like God and family, good health and good relationships and spend time on where and what there is value.

- Review your life goals, dreams and visions, let go off those that are no longer realistic or desirable even if still attainable (like your dream to own a sports car or wear size 8). Hold on to and fulfil those dreams that really matter. Do not allow regret for those things or people you had to let go, focus and value those that were left. Reignite and rediscover your purpose and embark on fulfilling it passionately and zealously.

- At this decade you do not need a romantic relationship or marriage to prove that you are desirable, because you are already confident in who you are and secure in your self-identity. So, if you do meet someone designed for you, then by all means embrace it (but for the right reasons)

5. YOUR SENSATIONAL SIXTIES

A Decade Characterized by Your Groundedness, Generosity and Graciousness)

"60 may not be the new 40 or 50, like everybody says, but you redefine 60, make it fabulously all your own." (Unknown)

During this decade most women's Calling has become forefront in terms of their focus and energy (before their career, profession and business) because most women are beginning to retire from what they had considered to be their job and work and have transitioned to their passion and purpose.

You cannot be written off at 60, because you are still of great public interest, you are bolder and louder in a good way, intense and deep with a voice and a message.

In your 60's you are content with what you have received and could not care less about what you have not achieved because wisdom dictates that you now sit back and enjoy your gains. Assess and write-off, your losses and consolidate the bricks that will cements your legacy which you need to build before the end of this decade, with what you have.

In your 60's you will develop a deep passion for something outside of yourself and it is in this decade that a sense of personal social responsibility and a deep desire to give back to society develops. This is a time also where you rely a lot on your social relationships more for fun and for charitable activities, you are more passionate about things like church clubs, social groups etc.

In your 60's you are very comfortable with yourself, you have learnt to be alone without being lonely. You have no time for vain superfluous goals or any need to prove yourself to anyone and you now focus on what really matters, that you can be remembered for.

If you had not given up high heels in your fifties, you now do so willingly. You have no apologies to make when you sit down at cocktails and exhibitions etc. and you do not pretend to like what you do not like. You have finally embraced your age gracefully with a calm confidence.

The 3 G's that to seek to define you in your 60's namely: your groundedness, your generosity and your graciousness.

i)   **Your Groundedness**

"Get yourself grounded and you can navigate even the stormiest road in peace." By Steve Goodier

By this stage you have gone through and survived all the seasons of life weathered all manner of storms and come out standing tall with your feet firmly rooted on the ground, and you have learnt to have a sober view of life, level headedness and you are more thoughtful and reflective.

You are unaffected and indifferent to people's opinions of you and their inability to handle your greatness because you are finally grounded in who you are, what you are capable of, your value and relevance and you are beyond and above trying to convince people to like you or approve of you.

You have encountered enough humbling events in your life. Your spouse, children, family and friends have caused all the drama that needed to be caused and quite honestly there is nothing any of them can do that can shake or destabilize you.

"Being grounded if you don't learn how to ground yourself in the present moment, you will live like a slave to your emotions, rather than a master of them." Unknown

Your groundedness has affected your loved ones positively by imparting some stability upon them.

ii)   **Your Generosity (Be Generous)**

"Generosity; the habit of giving freely without expecting anything in return." By Tiffany Soucek

At this stage you do not have many wants or needs and you are therefore more generous with your time, advice, wisdom, counsel etc. without needing to be paid back, recognized or applauded. You are more generous with your voice and opinion with a sincere desire to influence others positively.

"We make a living by what we get, but we make a life by what we give." By Winstone Churchill

At the same time having given your family and loved ones as much as you have over the decades, you now feel the need to widen your horizons and generously give yourself to a wider circle of people, and have a wide outreach over a larger jurisdiction.

"A kind gesture can reach a wound that only compassion can heal." By Steve Maraboli

iii)   **Your Graciousness**

"Your graciousness is what carries you. It isn't how old you are, how young you are, how beautiful you are or how short your skirt is, it is what comes out of your heart. If you are gracious, you have won the game" (Stevie Nicks)

Graciousness is marked by kindness, courtesy, tact, delicacy, charm, good taste and generosity of spirit. At 60, there is no more stress or struggle to get ahead and any temptation to be deceitful or manipulative is easily thwarted, by your maturity, graciousness and tolerance.

A gracious woman respects and honors others. She holds herself to a higher standard than that to which she holds others around her and she endeavors to live up to that measure. So, in your 60's you are grateful that you lived this long and you are genuinely grateful for so much in your life and you do not take anything for granted because you know many that did not have the grace to make it this far. Your gratitude makes you graciously accommodating, it makes you gentle in handling people and it makes you genuine in your feelings and actions, more emphatic and forgiving and certainly less critical and judgmental of others. In your 60's your grey hair is an honor and a mark of your wisdom.

Advise to Women in their Sensational Sixties

- Ensure you have clarity that the transition you are making from your work and job to your passion and purpose is clear and timely. Any confusion will mean that you will be mediocre in the job and work, and in your Calling and Purpose.

- At this stage you should start succession planning no matter how capable and energetic you are feeling.

- Do not despise what you have accomplished so far, consolidate your gains towards your legacy instead of straining and striving to create next complex dreams visions, focus on finishing and perfecting the ones you already have, so that you do it excellently.

- Listen to your body and be kind to it. Be deliberate about your health and wellness and be wise and sensible about self-care.

6. YOUR SERENE SEVENTIES

A Decade Characterized by Your Significance, Sagacity and Supremacy

Clearly at this stage most women's Destiny is a highlight and their Calling is already becoming a foundation for the legacy they are building.

Serene is being calm, peaceful, untroubled and tranquil. 7 is the number of completion meaning you have done your part and ran your race. It also symbolizes perfection, meaning you have come to an expected end after running your race faithfully, because as the Bible implies 70 is the end of a season of a man's life.

In your 70's you are supreme, spacious, stately, significant and all together splendid. You have developed capacity for pain and bliss all in one, you have developed resilience and being happy has become an acquired skill and a choice. You have an aptitude for appreciating life. Your happiness is built on attitude and it is intentional and deliberate.

By this decade most women have already shifted from being successful to being significant where they've more or less attained their goals and dreams or at least substantially and are no longer obsessed with making money or building empires and instead they desire to make significant contributions to their people, society and Nation.

During this decade people will begin to look at you in terms of your impact and your influence, your footprints and the legacy you are building.

In your 70's you are a phenomenal woman of substance, you have reasonable expectations but not demands, your joys and sorrows are so intertwined because you have had all the tragedy and all the bliss that life had to offer.

Your 70's can either be your decade of famine or your decade of plenty physically, emotionally and spiritually depending on how you conducted your other decades.

There are **3 S's** that seek to define you in your 70's namely: your significance, your sagacity, your supremacy.

Psalms 90:10 – The days of our lives *are* seventy years; And if by reason of strength *they are* eighty years, yet their boast *is* only labour and sorrow; For it is soon cut off, and we fly away.

i)   **Your Significance**

"Don't worry about being successful but work toward being significant and success will follow naturally." By Oprah Winfrey

Your legacy that is already impacting many makes you significant, and history records your impact as relevant and your society and nation are grateful that you lived. You have become worthy of attention and importance and a woman of substance.

"The more you celebrate and praise your life, the more there is in life to celebrate." By Oprah Winfrey

Your footprints should be evident and visible in your sphere of influence, for all to see that you were there and that you left a positive mark.

ii)   **Your Sagacity**

"Good judgment is as the result of experience and experience the result of bad judgment." By Mark Twain

Having lived this far, you are recognized for your wisdom, discernment and good judgment and since you are still senile you still have a lot to offer and you are still a great influence.

"It is only the prudence, sagacity, and much dexterity, that great aims are accomplished and all obstacles surmounted. Otherwise, nothing is accomplished." By Napoleon Bonaparte

It is true that this decade can also come with unfortunate afflictions and physical ailment, yet we serve a faithful and sustaining God.

iii)   **Your Supremacy**

"Authority doesn't always come from the loudest voice, but the wisest." By J.R. Morales

In your 70's you carry undisputed dominion and authority and you command respect and honor, not just because you are older, but because your maker deemed it necessary for you to remain here this long for a purpose.

You have a supremacy and distinction by virtue of the decades you have transcended.

Advice to Women in Their Serene Seventies

- Focus on consolidating the building bricks for the creation of your legacy because this is the stage where most women will be very clear as to the impact they have made and the legacy it will create.

- Forget about material wealth if you have not got it by now and focus on making a difference, leaving a legacy by impacting lives.

- Author books from your experience and let others learn valuable lessons from not only your successes but also from your failures.

- Stand Tall and choose to see just how complete and perfected you are because of this far you have come.

7. YOUR ELEGANT EIGHTIES

A Decade that defines you as a Living Legend, a Leading Lady and a Luminary

"Life is no brief candle to me. It is a sort of splendid torch which I have got hold of for the moment, and I want to make it burn as brightly as possible before handing it on to future generations" **Warren Bennis**

In terms of Destiny most women should have finished their race or are about to finish it and their legacy should be very visible and clear.

The number 8 symbolizes new beginnings i.e., transitions to another life. In your 80's you are larger than life and though frail physically and mentally weak you are still a force to be reckoned with in your family and society.

"Woman in their 80's are at their best because they always think they may be doing it for the last time" ~Unknown

In your 80's you are of tremendous value to your family and community (and though sometimes underestimated), your presence is powerful and awe striking and your quotes are powerful. It is a time of rewards and accolades because you have ran your race and finished it well. Your beauty is now on the inside, a precious inner beauty that makes your exterior even more attractive.

The **3 L's** that seek to define you in your 80's are namely: you are a living legend, a leading lady and a Luminary.

i)   **A Living Legend**

"Pursuit of your personal legend is your responsibility to life to give to the world the unique gift you were born to give and to become the person you were meant to become." Unknown

A legend is one who leaves behind an unforgettable impression on others. One who touches lives and is remembered and cherished. As a legend it means you found your Purpose and Calling and you fulfilled it.

You are alive and you are more or less running your race and you are at the finish and your impact and legacy are evident. So, to that extent you are indeed a legend, who is still alive for people to acknowledge and appreciate. Your part is to receive the accolades and acknowledgments graciously.

The fact that you are a living legend will define you positively because of doing something extremely well.

"Mothers are legendary for being able to read the thoughts of their children at just the right moment." Vivian Vande Velde

    ii)   **Leading Lady**

"You are supposed to be the leading lady of your own life." Unknown

You are a leading lady because you have left a mark of commendable leadership either in your family, community, business, sphere of influence or Nation.

Women in their eighties are of honor and there should be a standing ovation for them whenever they enter a room, a recognition and appreciation of this far you have come.

"If your actions create a legacy that inspires others to dream more, do more, become more, then you are an excellent leader" (Dolly Parton)

In addition, you have led the way and can still lead the way especially in your family, society and nation without any questions as to your ability and good will.

"As a leader it is a major responsibility on your shoulders to practice the behavior you want others to follow" ~ Himanshin Bhatia

    iii)   **A Luminary**

"A candle loses nothing by lighting another." ~James Keller

At 80, you pass on the torch to the next generation and let them build on the good foundations you have laid.

"The best leader's mentor and pass on the baton to worthy successors" ~ Unknown

In this decade you are definitely a shining star and a leading light of truth to many because you have done life and mastered it, by achieving success in the sphere you were sent to shine light on.

You have seen the darkness and the light and have the capacity to distinguish between the two and to aspire people to seek to walk in the light and truth.

"Be the beacon of light in someone's darkness." ~ Randi G. Fine

You are a pillar of justice, fairness and equality and you can be trusted, to stand for what is right and your experience goes ahead and testifies for you, and you can shed light on many issues to guide those behind you.

Advise to Women in their Elegant Eighties

- Since you may not have much physical energy and mental agility during this decade, then it is crucial for you to enjoy the fruits that come with having fulfilled your Purpose and Calling faithfully and to allow yourself to be recognized and celebrated.

- Do not fade away because you are still relevant and valuable.

- Do not muzzle your voice because it's still influential.

- Do not underestimate your inward strength emotionally and mentally even though outwardly you may appear frail.

- However, agree to relinquish responsibilities and duties to those you have been preparing for this time. Trust that you prepared them well and that they have what it takes.

"Create your legacy and pass on the baton" Billie Jean King

- Avoid stubbornly holding on and wanting to remain in control and in charge beyond your time, lest you spoil that which you had done so well.

- Allow people to help you and spoil you and baby you because you deserve it.

Destiny Questions to Ponder On

1. *Which factor do you believe defined you in your trendy twenties?*

2. *If you are already past your thriving thirties, what one factor tended to define you in your thirties that you now wish hadn't? If you are currently in your thriving thirties, what factors do you think should define you?*

3. *If you are already past your formidable forties, how secure would you say your identity was in that decade and what factors made it secure?*
   If you are currently in your formidable forties, do you believe you are now more self-secure than you were and if so what has contributed to this self-security?

4. *How does success or lack of it affect a woman's identity during her feisty fifties and to what extent do you think it should or should not?*

5. *What in your opinion would you wish to have accomplished by the end of your sensational sixties decade?*
   If you are already in this or past this decade, what one thing had you hoped to accomplish by now that you haven't?

6. *Would you expect self-security to be automatic in your serene seventies decade and if not, what factors do you think might threaten one's self-security in this decade?*

7. *What would be your most important desire or wish in your elegant eighties decade? What legacy do you want to leave?*

WORDS HAVE POWER

Relevant Quotes and Scripture Meditations

for Your Harvests and Legacy

Inspirational Quotes and Scriptures about the Woman of Destiny

"*Strong women not only feel pain, they accept it, they learn from it and fight through it. They turn their wounds into wisdom. They may fall, but they always get back up, dust off, and fight like they have never fought before.*" By **Unknown**

"*A woman who is at rest with herself has nothing to prove to others, she embraces her strengths & cheers others on with a pure heart. Her light shines brightly; her words are seasoned with kindness, goodness & grace. She is peaceful & edifies others as she is secure in her Heavenly Father.*" By **Hanna Bryant**

"*God has a purpose for your pain, a reason for your struggle and a reward for your faithfulness. Trust Him and don't give.*" By **Dave Willis**

"*She may be quiet, but she's a warrior and her prayers can move mountains.*" **Unknown**

"*She is not broken anymore, she is stronger, wiser and more beautiful than before, because God took her broken pieces and made her new again.*" By **Unknown**

"*Though my soul may set in darkness, it will rise in perfect light; I have loved the stars too fondly to be fearful of the night.*" By **Sarah Williams**

"*In the end, she became more than she was expected. She became the journey, and like all journeys, she did not end, she just simply changed directions and kept going.*" By **R.M. Drake**

"Mirror! Mirror! on the wall, I'll always get up after I fall. And whether I run, walk or have to crawl, I'll set my goals and achieve them all." By **Brie Edison**

"I am a strong woman because a strong woman raised me." By **Unknown**

"We all have an unsuspected reserve of strength inside that emerges when life puts us to test." By **Isabel Allende**

"Keep your head up. God gives his hardest battles to his strongest soldiers." By **Unknown**

"If you feel like you are losing everything, remember that trees lose their leaves every year and they still stand tall and wait for better days to come." By **Unknown**

"Strength grows in the moments when you think you can't go on, but you keep going anyway." By **Unknown**

"Some women are lost in the fire. Some women are built from it." By **Michelle K**

"I know you're tired, you're fed up, you're so close to breaking, but there is strength within you even when you feel weak. Keep fighting. By **Unknown**

"Strength doesn't come from what you can do. It comes from overcoming the things you once thought you couldn't. By **Rikki Rogers**

"It's actually pretty simple. Either you do it, or you don't." By **Unknown**

"She believed she could, so she did." By **R.S. Grey**

"I'm proud of the woman I am because I went through one hell of a time becoming her." By **Unknown**

"The circles of women in our lives weave invisible nets of love that carry us when we are weak, and they sing with us when we are strong." By **Sark**

"Behind every successful woman is a tribe of other successful women, who have her back." By **Kimberly**

"Women should empower each other, instead of being so hateful and envious of one another." By **Unknown**

"A successful woman is one who can build a firm foundation with the bricks others have thrown to her." By **Unknown**

"It took me quite a long time to develop a voice, and now that I have it I am not going to be silent." By **Madeleine Albright**

"She overcomes everything that was meant to destroy her." By **Sylvester McNutt III**

"When women support each other, incredible things happen." By **Viola Davis**

"Each time a woman stands up for herself, she stands up for all women." By **Maya Angelou**

"A woman is unstoppable after she realizes she deserves better." By **Yene D.**

"I am obsessed with seeing women encourage, support, and empower other women. It's my favorite, we need more of it." By **Unknown**

"I would like to be known as an intelligent woman, a courageous woman, a loving woman, a woman who teaches by being." By **Maya Angelou**

"Here's to strong women, may we know them, may we be them, may we raise them." By **Unknown**

"She never seemed shattered; to me she was the breathtaking mosaic of the battles she won." By **Unknown**

"A strong woman, looks a challenge in the eye, and gives it a wink." By **Gina Carey**

"Never underestimate the power of a kind woman. Kindness is a choice that comes from incredible strength." By **Unknown**

"She surrounds herself with women she can grow with." By **Unknown**

"When a woman is loved correctly, she becomes ten times, the woman she was before." By **Unknown**

"A woman unaffected by insult has made her enemies absolutely powerless." By **Entity**

"A strong woman in her essence is a gift to the world." By **Unknown**

"I want every girl to know that her voice can change the world." By **Malala Yousafzai**

"Women who compliment other women genuinely are a whole different breed. Real Queens" By **Unknown**

"Nothing is more impressive than a woman who is secure in the unique way God made her." By **Rhonda Kulczyk**

"Empowered women empower women." By **Unknown**

"A foolish woman keeps talking, a wise woman understands the power of her words as well as her silence." By **Unknown**

"And one day she discovered, that she was fierce, and strong, and full of fire, and that not even she could hold herself back, because her passion burned brighter than her fears." By **Mark Anthony**

"We need women who are so strong, they can be gentle, so educated they can be humble, so fierce they can be compassionate, so passionate they can be rational, and so disciplined they can be free." By **Kavita N. Ramdas**

"A strong woman is a woman determined to do something others are determined not to be done." By **Marge Piercy**

"Be strong enough to let go, and wise enough to wait for what you deserve." By **Unknown**

"Strong women lift each other up." By **Unknown**

"A woman is like a tea bag, you never know how strong it is until it is in hot water." By **Eleanor Roosevelt**

"A strong woman is one, who feels deeply and loves fiercely, her tears flow just as abundantly as her laughter. A strong woman is both soft and powerful, she is both practical and spiritual, a strong woman in her essence is a gift to the world." By **Unknown**

"Strong women wear their pain like stilettos, no matter how much it hurts, all you see is the beauty of it. By **Harriet Morgan**

"Success isn't about how much money you make, it's about the difference you make in people's lives." By **Michelle Obama**

"To attract money, you must focus on wealth. It is impossible, to bring more money into your life, when you are noticing you don't have enough because that means you are thinking thoughts that you don't have enough." By **Rhonda Byrne**

"You can only become truly accomplished at something you love. Don't make money your goal. Instead pursue the things you love doing and then do them so well that people can't take their eyes off you." By **Maya Angelou**

"Here's to financially independent Women, may we know them, may we be them, may we raise them." By **Unknown**

"People, who have drawn wealth into their lives, used the secret consciously or unconsciously, they think thoughts of abundance of wealth, and they don't allow any contradictory to take roots in their minds." By **Rhonda Byrne**

"Save your money and one day your money will save you." By **Unknown**

"Nearly every glamorous, wealthy, successful career woman, you might envy now, started out as some kind of schlep. By **Helen Gurley Brown**

"A business career for a woman, and her needs for a woman's life, as wife and mother, are not enemies at all, unless we make them so. But maybe the closest and most co-operative friends and supporters of each other." By **Hortense Oldum**

"Leadership is about making others better as a result of your presence and making sure that impact lasts in your absence." By **Sheryl Sandberg**

"Women need to shift from thinking I'm not ready to do that to I'll learn by doing it." By **Sheryl Sandberg**

"If your actions create a legacy that inspires others to dream more, learn more, do more and become more, then, you are an excellent leader." By **Dolly Parton**

"I just want women to always feel in control, because we are capable, we're so capable." By **Nicki Minaj**

"A leader takes people where they want to go. A great leader takes people where they don't necessarily want to go, but ought to be." By **Rosalynn Carter**

"Because I am a woman, I must make unusual effort to succeed. If I fail, no one will say, 'She doesn't have what it takes.' They will say, women don't have what it takes." By **Unknown**

"Our deepest fear is not that we are inadequate. Our deepest fear is that we are powerful beyond measure." By **Marianne Williamson**

"Leadership is hard to define and good leadership even harder. But if you can get people to follow you to the end of the earth, you are a great leader." By **Indra Nooyi**

"People respond well to those that are sure of what they want." By **Anna Wintour**

"No power on earth compares to a mother's tender prayer." By **Edwin Arnold**

"I remember my mother's prayer and they have always followed me. They have clung to me all my life." By **Abraham Lincoln**

"The battle for our children's lives is waged on our knees." By **Stormie Omartian**

"Prayer warrior mothers cover their kids with God's blessings and protection." By **Marla Alupoaicei**

"Every mother's prayer; guide her to a place where she'll be safe." By **Carole Bayer Sager**

"The bond between mothers and their children is one defined by love. As a mother's prayer for her children are unending, so are the wisdom, grace and strength they provide for their children." By **President George W. Bush**

"God does hear and answer prayers… From childhood, at my mother's knee where I first learned to pray . . . I know without question that it is possible for men and women to reach out in humility and prayer and tap that Unseen Power." ~**Ezra Taft Benson**

"During all those years of struggle and heartache, my mother never worried. She took all her troubles to God in prayer." ~**Dale Carnegie**

"My mother knew when to listen and when to pray and when to help. I wonder how many people knew the compassion [my mother] held for them and how hard, in the privacy of her God Box, she prayed for them and their struggles." ~**Mary Lou Quinlan**

"To this day, even though I am grown and have two children of my own, whenever I travel somewhere distant or am undertaking a major project, my mother will sit me down, lay hands on me, and say a prayer of blessing." ~**Francisco J. García** Jr.

"From the time of my earliest memories, she impressed upon me one rule above all others: when I woke from sleep, my first duty was to pray to God for spiritual nourishment and blessings . . . my mother would never relent . . . She planted in me, and tended in my early life, a profound love and fear of God." ~**Sadhu Sundar Singh**

Bible Wisdom about the Woman of Destiny

Proverbs 31:30; "Charm is deceitful and beauty is passing, But a woman who fears the LORD, she shall be praised."

Psalm 46:5 "God is in the midst of her, she shall not be moved; God shall help her, just at the break of dawn."

Proverbs 31:16-17 "She considers a field and buys it; from her profits she plants a vineyard. She girds herself with strength, and strengthens her arms."

1 Corinthians 15:10 "But by the grace of God I am what I am, and His grace toward me was not in vain; but I labored more abundantly than they all, yet not I, but the grace of God *which was* with me."

Proverbs 31:20-21 "She extends her hand to the poor, Yes, she reaches out her hands to the needy. She is not afraid of snow for her household, For all her household *is* clothed with scarlet."

Psalm 139:14 "I will praise You, for I am fearfully and wonderfully made; Marvellous are Your works, And that my soul knows very well."

1 Corinthians 11:12 "For as woman came from man, even so man also comes through woman; but all things are from God."

1 Peter 3:3-4 "Do not let your adornment be merely outward—arranging the hair, wearing gold, or putting on fine apparel—rather let it be the hidden person of the heart, with the incorruptible beauty of a gentle and quiet spirit, which is very precious in the sight of God."

1 Timothy 3:11 "Likewise, their wives must be reverent, not slanderers, temperate, faithful in all things."

Luke 1:45 "Blessed is she who believed that there will be a fulfilment of those things which were told her from the Lord."

Proverbs.31:20 "She extends her hand to the poor, Yes, she reaches out her hands to the needy."

Proverbs 11:16 "A gracious woman retains honor, But ruthless *men* retain riches."

Proverbs 31:25 "Strength and honor *are* her clothing; She shall rejoice in time to come."

Proverbs 3:15 "She *is* more precious than rubies, And all the things you may desire cannot compare with her."

Proverbs 31:26 "She opens her mouth with wisdom, And on her tongue *is* the law of kindness."

Proverbs. 14:1 "The wise woman builds her house, But the foolish pulls it down with her hands.

Proverbs. 19:13 "A foolish son is the ruin of his father, And the contentions of a wife are a continual dripping."

Proverbs. 21:9 "Better to dwell in a corner of a housetop, Than in a house shared with a contentious woman."

Proverbs. 31: 17-18 "She girds herself with strength, And strengthens her arms. She perceives that her merchandise is good, And her lamp does not go out by night."

Proverbs.21:19 "Better to dwell in the wilderness, Than with a contentious and angry woman."

Proverbs. 31: 16 "She considers a field and buys it; From her profits she plants a vineyard."

Proverbs.12:4 "An excellent wife is the crown of her husband, But she who causes shame is like rottenness in his bones."

Proverbs. 31:19 "She stretches out her hands to the distaff, And her hand holds the spindle.

Proverbs. 31:10-12 "Who can find a virtuous wife? For her worth is far above rubies. The heart of her husband safely trusts her; So he will have no lack of gain. She does him good and not evil All the days of her life."

Proverbs. 31:13-15 "She seeks wool and flax, And willingly works with her hands. She is like the merchant ships, She brings her food from afar. She also rises while it is yet night, And provides food for her household, And a portion for her maidservants."

Proverbs.31:26 "She opens her mouth with wisdom, And on her tongue is the law of kindness."

Ephesians.5:22-23 "Wives, submit to your own husbands, as to the Lord. For the husband is head of the wife, as also Christ is head of the church; and He is the Saviour of the body."

1st Peter. 3:1-2 "Wives, likewise, be submissive to your own husbands, that even if some do not obey the word, they, without a word, may be won by the conduct of their wives, when they observe your chaste conduct accompanied by fear."

Titus. 2:3-5 "The older women likewise, that they be reverent in behaviour, not slanderers, not given to much wine, teachers of good things— that they admonish the young women to love their husbands, to love their children to be discreet, chaste, homemakers, good, obedient to their own husbands, that the word of God may not be blasphemed."

1ˢᵗ Tim. 2:9-10 "In like manner also, that the women adorn themselves in modest apparel, with propriety and moderation, not with braided hair or gold or pearls or costly clothing, but, which is proper for women professing godliness, with good works."

1ˢᵗ Cor. 11:3 "But I want you to know that the head of every man is Christ, the head of woman is man, and the head of Christ is God."

1ˢᵗ Tim.5:14 "Therefore I desire that the younger widows marry, bear children, manage the house, give no opportunity to the adversary to speak reproachfully."

Col.3:18-19 "Wives, submit to your own husbands, as is fitting in the Lord. Husbands, love your wives and do not be bitter toward them."

Proverbs.31:27 "She watches over the ways of her household, And does not eat the bread of idleness."

2ⁿᵈ Tim.1:5 "when I call to remembrance the genuine faith that is in you, which dwelt first in your grandmother Lois and your mother Eunice, and I am persuaded is in you also."

Proverbs.31:28 "Her children rise up and call her blessed; Her husband also, and he praises her."

Proverbs.31:25 "Strength and honour are her clothing; She shall rejoice in time to come."

Proverbs 18:22 "He who finds a wife finds a good thing, And obtains favour from the LORD."

Proverbs.23:22 "Listen to your father who begot you, And do not despise your mother when she is old."

Proverbs.4:6 "Do not forsake her, and she will preserve you; Love her, and she will keep you."

Proverbs.11:22 "As a ring of gold in a swine's snout, So is a lovely woman who lacks discretion."

Proverbs.31:21 "She is not afraid of snow for her household, For all her household is clothed with scarlet."

BIBLIOGRAPHY

The Bible

Jakes, T.D.2002.*God's Leading Lady: Out of the Shadows and into the Light.* Berkley.

Sandberg, Sheryl & Scovell, Nell.2013.*Lean In: Women, Work, and the Will to Lead.* Alfred A. Knopf.

Stigel, V. Herta.2011.*The Mountain Within: Leadership Lessons and Inspiration for Your Climb to the Top.* McGraw-Hill Eductaion.

Scott, Janny.2011.*A Singular Woman: The Untold Story of Barack Obama's Mother.* Riverhead Books.

Meyer, Joyce.2010.*Eat the Cookie... Buy the Shoes: Giving Yourself Permission to Lighten Up.* FaithWords.

Karssen, Gien.1974.*Her Name is Woman.* NavPress Publishing Group.

Live By Faith by Rev. Teresa Wairimu

Yancey, Philip.2002.*Where Is God When It Hurts?* Zondervan.

Shellenberger, Susie & Gowler, Kathy.2007.*What Your Daughter Isn't Telling You: Expert Insight Into the World of Teen Girls.* Bethany House Publishers.

Boundaries by Pastor Sammy Hinn

Covey, R. Stephen.2004.*The 7 Habits of Highly Effective People: Powerful Lessons in Personal Change.* Free Press.

Dr. D. W. Ekstrand, 2012. The Influence Parents have on their Children. Accessed on 28th July, 2020 http://www.thetransformedsoul.com/additional-studies

Sasha, 2016: The influence of a good teacher can never be erased. Accessed on 28th July, 2020 https://mirrorgirlblog.wordpress.com/2016/09/17/

Leslie Becker-Phelps, PHD, 2005; Ways your Friends Influence your Future. Accessed on https://blogs.webmd.com/relationships/20160928

Brandon Thomas, 2008: Does past experience affect what we see or what we do? accessed on 29th July, 2020 https://www.researchgate.net/post/Does_past_experience

Art Markman, Ph.D. 2011: Your View of the Future Is Shaped by the Past. Accessed on 29th July, 2020 https://www.psychologytoday.com/us/blog/ulterior-motives/201108

Orit E. Tykocinski and Andreas Ortmann. 2011: The Lingering Effects of Our Past Experiences: The Sunk-Cost Fallacy and the Inaction-Inertia Effect. Accessed on 29th July, 2020 http://portal.idc.ac.il/he/schools/psychology/

Claire Newton. 2020: Destiny: Action or Accident? Accessed on 29th July 2020 http://www.clairenewton.co.za/my-articles/destiny-action-or-accident.html

Sandra Dawes.2014. Following your inner voice. Accessed on 29th July, 2020 https://embraceurdestiny.com/2014/01/29/

following-your-inner-voice/

Kenneth Copeland, 2018. Ways to Know If You're Hearing God's Voice. Accessed on 29th July,2020 https://blog.kcm.org/4-ways-know-youre-hearing-gods-voice/

Pincott Jena E, 2019. Silencing Your Inner Critic, accessed on 29th July, 2020 https://www.psychologytoday.com/us/articles/201903/silencing-your-inner-critic

Bonnie Badenoch, Ph.D. 2010. Critical Inner Voice. Accessed on 29th July, 2020 https://www.psychalive.org/critical-inner-voice/

BIBLIOGRAPHY